EXECUTIVE LEADERSHIP

IN THE PUBLIC SERVICE

EXECUTIVE LEADERSHIP
IN THE PUBLIC SERVICE

EDITED BY ROBERT B. DENHARDT
AND WILLIAM H. STEWART

THE UNIVERSITY OF ALABAMA PRESS

Tuscaloosa and London

Copyright © 1992 by
The University of Alabama Press
Tuscaloosa, Alabama 35487–0380
All rights reserved
Manufactured in the United States of America

∞

The paper on which this book is printed meets the minimum
requirements of American National Standard for Information
Science-Permanence of Paper for Printed Library Materials,
ANSI Z39.48-1984.

Library of Congress Cataloging-in-Publication Data

Executive leadership in the public service / edited by Robert B.
  Denhardt and William H. Stewart.
      p.   cm.
  Includes bibliographical references and index.
  ISBN 0-8173-0571-8
  1. Presidents—United States. 2. Governors—United States.
3. City managers—United States. 4. Political leadership—United
States.   I. Denhardt, Robert B.   II. Stewart, William H.
JK518.E94   1992
350.003'13'0973—dc20   91-32950

British Library Cataloguing-in-Publication Data available

Dedicated to the Memory of
Coleman B. Ransone, Jr.
(1920–1986)

CONTENTS

INTRODUCTION: ESSAYS IN MEMORY OF
COLEMAN B. RANSONE, JR.
Robert B. Denhardt and William H. Stewart   1

1. POLITICAL PROFESSIONALISM
   Charles T. Goodsell   7

2. FINDING THE PUBLIC IN PUBLIC ADMINISTRATION
   H. George Frederickson   20

3. PUBLIC LEADERSHIP: A DEVELOPMENTAL PERSPECTIVE
   Robert B. Denhardt and Kevin Prelgovisk   33

4. POLITICAL STRATEGY FOR THE POSTMODERN PRESIDENCY
   Ryan J. Barilleaux   45

5. PRESIDENTIAL PERSUASIVENESS AND PUBLIC SECTOR
   LEADERSHIP
   Marcia Lynn Whicker and Todd W. Areson   64

6. FEDERALISM AND ADMINISTRATIVE DISCRETION
   William H. Stewart   81

7. GUBERNATORIAL LEADERSHIP AND STATE
   ADMINISTRATION: INSTITUTIONAL ORIENTATIONS
   IN A CHANGING POLITICAL ENVIRONMENT
   Cheryl M. Miller and Deil S. Wright   95

8. THE CHANGED POLICY CONTEXT OF THE STATES; OR,
   WHY GREAT INDIVIDUALS OUGHT NOW TO BE
   ELECTED GOVERNOR
   Donald T. Wells   119

9. A NEW PROFESSIONALISM IN CITY MANAGEMENT
   John Nalbandian   137

CONCLUSION
   William H. Stewart and Robert B. Denhardt 153

References 161

Contributors 173

Index 177

EXECUTIVE LEADERSHIP
IN THE PUBLIC SERVICE

INTRODUCTION: ESSAYS IN MEMORY OF COLEMAN B. RANSONE, JR.

Robert B. Denhardt and William H. Stewart

The essays in this volume were commissioned in memory of Coleman B. Ransone, Jr., a longtime faculty member in the Department of Political Science at The University of Alabama and, for many years, director of the Southern Regional Training Program (SRTP) in Public Administration. Professor Ransone ("Ranse" as many called him) was a gifted teacher, concerned not only that his students acquire knowledge but that they develop the skills and maturity necessary to pursue successful careers in the public service. Equally important, however, Professor Ransone was among the most active early scholars to apply the tools of modern social science to questions of executive leadership, especially at the state level. For the authors of these essays, and for many others, Coleman Ransone served as a mentor, friend, or model for scholarly achievement. This volume stands as a tribute to all he left us.

Coleman Ransone, Jr., was born on January 17, 1920, in Norfolk, Virginia. He did his undergraduate work at the College of William and Mary, graduating in 1941. While at William and Mary he was tapped for membership in Phi Beta Kappa. At the outset of World War II he served as a personnel technician in the Office for Emergency Management. From 1943 to 1946, he was a member of the U.S. Army Air Force. After the war he went to Harvard University, where he earned his M.P.A. degree in 1947 and his Ph.D. in 1950. Before finishing his Ph.D., Ransone joined the University of Alabama faculty as a member of the Department of Political Science. He remained in Tuscaloosa for the rest of his academic career with the exception of one year back at his undergraduate alma mater. Ransone's long tenure as director of the Southern Regional Training Program began in 1953. His work with the program brought him much deserved recognition. He served on the executive committee of the National Association of Schools of Public Affairs and Administration (NASPAA) in 1962–63. *Public Administration Review* and the *International Journal of Public Administration* benefited from his expertise when he was a member of their editorial boards. Within the state of Alabama, Professor Ransone was also very active. In 1969–70 he was a consultant to the Alabama Ethics Commission. This association led to a publication, *Ethics in Alabama State Government*. At the same time, he also began several years' service as a member of the Alabama Constitutional Commission, which, with his significant contribution, produced the draft for a new state constitution. Its prospects for adoption were moderately favorable until George Wallace was returned to office. Ransone was active in promoting the study of political science in Alabama and was an early president of the Alabama Political Science Association. He retired from teaching on February 1, 1985. Before his death at age sixty-six on July 11, 1986, the lectureship that had been such an important part of the SRTP was renamed in his honor.

Professor Ransone's interest in questions of executive leadership was reflected in a large number of publications, most notably his works on the American governorship. Already well-known for his study *The Office of Governor in the South* (1951), in 1956 Professor Ransone completed a major study titled *The Office of Governor in the United States*, a volume that soon came to be regarded as a classic in gubernatorial studies. In the latter volume Ransone reported on a series of interviews with governors, members of the governors' staffs, department heads, legislators, and others knowledgeable about state government and especially the role of the governor. Ransone found that the governor's role consisted of three areas of operation—public relations (largely the partisan political role), policy formation (the creative aspect of governance), and management (the administrative aspect). Ransone revisited his work in a book titled *The American Governorship* (1982), an important reexamination of his earlier thesis.

As a substantial political leader in state government, Ransone pointed out, the governor faces many of the curious and conflicting demands placed on other public leaders. Ransone quoted James Forrestal approvingly: "The difficulty of Government work is that it not only has to be well done, but the public has to be convinced that it is being well done. In other words, there is a necessity for both competence and exposition, and I hold it is extremely difficult to combine the two in the same person" (quoted in Ransone, 1956:153). Ransone found the same dilemma facing the governor as a state leader. Thus the governor "must not only prepare a legislative program and see that it is enacted and establish administrative policies and see that they are adhered to, but he must constantly assure the citizens that these functions are being well done and that he is carrying out the promises which he made in the election" (Ransone, 1956:153).

The dilemma the governor faces in trying to combine competence and exposition, as well as responding to the differing demands of public relations, policy formation, and management, is a theme that runs through much of Ransone's work. But there is also a conviction that individuals can be found—or can be developed—who will successfully undertake the important role(s) of public leadership. In this way, Ransone's scholarship met his commitment to education for the public service. Nowhere was that commitment more clearly demonstrated than in Ransone's work with the Southern Regional Training Program.

The SRTP had been initiated in 1943 in an effort to bring the resources of three great southern universities (originally Alabama, Tennessee, and Georgia but ultimately Alabama, Tennessee, and Kentucky) and those of emerging public agencies at the federal, state, and local levels to bear on the question of professionalizing the public service in the South. The SRTP program was one of the earliest graduate programs in public administration in the region and was unique in its multiuniversity involvement. There is no question but that the SRTP program contributed substantially toward building a highly professional public service throughout the South and indeed throughout the nation.

Students who went through the program recall many talented faculty—Albert Lepawsky, Roscoe Martin, York Willbern, Gladys Kammerer, Robert Highsaw, Lee Greene, Malcolm Jewell, and many others. But they had special affection for Coleman Ransone, for it was Ransone who recruited most of them to the program, who worked with them closely to establish effective internship experiences, and who monitored (and mentored) their various academic pursuits. Most of all, Ransone was a friend to all who came in contact with the program during the many years he directed it and was the one who most consistently earned their high regard and esteem.

It is our hope that the essays in this volume accurately mirror Coleman Ransone's interests in the analysis of and preparation for public leadership. The book first deals with the changing context of public leadership and with how our thinking about leadership in the public service might be improved. We also give attention to ways the leadership capabilities of those in the public service might be enhanced. Next we turn to a somewhat more practical examination of leadership at the presidential level, the level at which public leadership today is most visible and potentially most impressive. Finally, following Ransone's lead, we turn to a consideration of executive leadership in the state and local arenas.

Charles T. Goodsell opens our volume with a quotation from Coleman Ransone to the effect that a central problem in democratic government is to combine strong leadership with real accountability. Goodsell argues that such a combination would be aided by the development of "political professionalism," applicable both to elected political leaders (such as presidents, governors, and mayors) and to top career people in government (agency directors, bureau chiefs, city managers, and the like). The key to Goodsell's idea of political professionalism is the recognition by these professionals that they belong to a privileged group that is entrusted with a powerful force for human betterment, the action of legitimated government. Toward this end, Goodsell urges that we consider the contribution to public leadership of a competence for power, a capacity for synthesis, an ability to exercise discretion within constraints, and the possession of a service ethic.

H. George Frederickson, also concerned with the ethical posture of public leaders, examines the evolving meaning of the term *public* in recent years, to the point that a concern for individual preferences may have all but eliminated any concept of the public realm other than that which equates the public interest with the accumulation of various private interests. Frederickson argues for the restoration of a more substantial recognition of public concerns and for a public administration that is not merely concerned with the administration of government agencies but rather with a responsible response to public interests wherever they may be found.

In their essay, Robert B. Denhardt and Kevin Prelgovisk address the nature and demands of leadership in contemporary society. Denhardt and Prelgovisk contend that the complexity of society requires creative solutions to the problems we face at all levels and that, in turn, leadership is desperately needed at all levels. This concept, which Denhardt and Prelgovisk term "public leadership," involves a reciprocal relationship between the leader and the group through which the shared interests of the members are articulated in an open and public process so as to provide direction and motivation for group action. Such leadership requires not only traditional management skills but also a set of skills related to discovering and articulating the group's latent interest, then acting as a "trigger" for group action.

From these general observations about the context of public leadership in contemporary society, we turn to leadership at the center of the American political system, the presidency. Ryan J. Barilleaux opens the discussion by delineating what he terms the "postmodern presidency," a mode of governing characterized by such features as the revival of presidential prerogative power (in such areas as foreign policy and the budget), the increasing use of "public politics" (something Ransone's work had also noted), and the growth of the Executive Office of the President as a presidential secretariat. Following his description of the postmodern presidency, Barilleaux discusses some strategies that presidents might use to enhance their executive leadership, advice that runs the gamut from seizing budget and policy initiatives to making the most of the prerogatives of the postmodern presidency.

Marcia Lynn Whicker and Todd W. Areson continue the discussion by focusing on the character of presidential "exposition," the way presidents have been successful in persuading Congress, the public, and the press to pursue their goals. Some of the issues examined relate to the persuasiveness of the message, others to the persuasiveness of the messenger. Whicker and Areson then develop a model of presidential persuasiveness that allows them to classify certain presidents as high on both dimensions (Roosevelt, Kennedy, and Reagan), others as low on both dimensions (Hoover, Carter, and Ford), and still others as high on one dimension and low on the other.

William H. Stewart shifts the discussion more clearly to the administrative role of the president and other generalist and specialist governmental actors, pointing out that effective leadership in modern society must take into account the shifting character of the intergovernmental system in which we operate. Stewart suggests several forms of federalism, among them dual federalism, cooperative federalism, national federalism, and the new federalism models of Presidents Nixon and Reagan. Stewart then discusses some of the implications of these models for the distribution of discretion in executive leadership throughout the intergovernmental system.

Our attention then shifts to the question of executive leadership at the state and local levels. Cheryl M. Miller and Deil S. Wright open the discussion by examining a topic very much in line with the interests of Coleman Ransone, the relationship between the governor and the administrative agencies of state government. Miller and Wright note first the dramatic growth in the size, scope, and diversity of state agencies over the past three decades, then examine changes in the office of governor from administrative figurehead to executive leader. Miller and Wright also note, however, that governors who attempt to exercise their increased executive powers often collide with state legislative bodies because changes and expansions have occurred there as well. Finally, the views of state administrators with respect to these trends are examined and found to be fairly stable over time with respect to gubernatorial and legislative influence.

Donald T. Wells examines another of Ransone's three areas of gubernatorial leadership, that of policy formation. Wells suggests that governors have substantially more influence in policy making than they used to have, though the policy of the governorship is more likely today than before to be characterized by issues that are intergenerational, international, and intergovernmental. Under contemporary conditions, Wells argues, the governor can and indeed must play a proactive role in the highly political process of developing public policy.

John Nalbandian's closing essay focuses on the executive leadership role of the city manager, but in doing so brings us full circle to the political and ethical concerns that opened the volume. Nalbandian points out that, though the political neutrality of city managers has long been a part of the council-manager form of government, today's managers have become policy advocates, negotiators of diverse interests, and consensus builders within their communities. Under such conditions, city managers may need to think more clearly about the values they represent in their work—values such as representativeness, efficiency, individual rights, and social equity. These values (the values of "political professionals"?), rather than the values of neutral competence, are likely to provide legitimation to future city managers in their role as executive leaders.

Coleman Ransone was sensitive to the need for executive leadership in the public service. But he was also sensitive to the need for leadership to be placed in the proper political and ethical context. We noted at the outset his work with the Alabama Ethics Commission. In this volume, we will explore a variety of topics of great practical significance in asserting public leadership in modern society. But we will also seek to demonstrate that leadership devoid of political and ethical concerns is ill-suited to the world of today and tomorrow. To the contrary, we join in the quest for new modes of executive leadership, balanced in their attention to power and to people, to public policy, public management, and public service.

1 POLITICAL PROFESSIONALISM

Charles T. Goodsell

Coleman B. Ransone, Jr., opened his classic work on the governorship with these words: "One of the central problems of democratic government is to devise a system by which there can be strong leadership combined with real accountability to the electorate. We must have responsible government if we are to have democratic government, but we must also have government capable of decisive action if our democracy is to survive in a world of antagonistic and competitive philosophies" (Ransone, 1956:vii).

Effective leadership in the public service, the subject of this volume, is a central means to strong but democratic government, not only in the state but at all levels of government. This chapter takes the position that effective governmental leadership is fostered by, among other factors, a concept of political professionalism. This term, which will sound strange to many, refers to a self-awareness on the part of elected and appointed leaders alike that they belong to a privileged group that is entrusted—temporarily—with directing the most powerful means of human betterment known to humankind, the collective and compulsory action of legitimated government. This awareness embodies, it is argued, a set of normative principles whose totality may be said to constitute a highly refined notion of professionalism.

These principles are a competence for power, a capacity for synthesis, an ability to exercise discretion within constraints, and possession of a service ethos. This chapter's thesis is that these principles can, are, and should be met in public service leadership. Political professionalism now exists in some places, I argue, and is a worthy ideal for all to pursue.

Reconsidering Traditional Ideas

Traditional thinking on politics and professionalism would dismiss the title of this chapter as an oxymoron. Many view the two spheres as widely separated and perhaps polar opposites. Politics is seen as the manipulation of power for the sake of expediency, while professionalism is viewed as serving others through expert knowledge. Politics is regarded as the pursuit of influence and governmental control by a band of rank amateurs who are willing to compromise on what is right in order to win. Professionalism is depicted as the application of certifiably correct knowledge, undisturbed by the influence of ignorant and self-regarding outsiders. The hostility between politics and professionalism is hence long-standing and ever-present, it is often concluded. In Frederick Mosher's words:

> There is a built-in aversion between the professions and politics. Its origin is historical: most of the professions, and particularly those in the public service category, won their professional spurs over many arduous years to the extent they could escape the infiltration, the domination, and the influence of politicians (who, to most professionals, are by definition amateurs at best and corrupt ones at worst). . . . The aversion to politics has contemporary supports. Professionalism rests upon specialized knowledge, science, and rationality. There are *correct* ways of solving problems and doing things. Politics is seen as constituting negotiation, elections, votes, compromises—all carried on by subject-matter amateurs. Politics is to the professions as ambiguity to truth, expediency to rightness, heresy to true belief. (1968:108–9)

Before I begin to reconcile this seeming contradiction between politics and professionalism in the manner intended, let me indicate ways in which I do *not* attempt to do so. By *political professionalism* I am not referring to the professionalization of political campaign work or the training of lobbyists, pollsters, and media experts. Several graduate programs in political management have sprung up around the country, and these regard the combination of political campaigning and public opinion polling as an emerging profession in its own right. Nor am I referring to the interest-group behavior of organized professions such as the American Bar Association or American Medical Association, or entry into politics by lawyers, scientists, engineers, and other professionals. These matters are essential to our understanding of pluralist democracy, but they do not relate to our subject.

The present theme is, rather, that executive leadership can itself be conceived as a profession. I contend that the top elected and appointed executives of a democratically constituted government—the "pols" if you will—can and should also be thought of as "pros," *if* they live up to certain standards of behavior. My category of top executives includes men and women customarily thought of as falling into two distinct categories: the "political people," such as elected chief executives—presidents, governors, and mayors, plus their senior advisers, cabinet officers, and top agency appointees; and the "career people"—civil servants who operate at the pinnacles of power in their agencies, in roles such as agency director, deputy and assistant director, bureau chief, chief counsel, senior staff officer, county administrator, and city manager.

These top political and career executives, together, are responsible for directing our executive branches of government, the administrations of presidents and governors and mayors and the administrative departments and agencies that do the actual work of governing. It is these individuals who, collectively, develop and propose policy, write legislative agendas, articulate policy options, lead administrative organizations, allocate scarce public resources, build or destroy agency morale, construct or dissipate external coalitions of support, provide vision or permit drift, and are held accountable for what is done by government and what happens to populations.

As the most elemental student of public administration knows, traditional thinking in democratic theory of bureaucracy makes a point of not treating these two groups of executives as one but instead of separating them. "Politicians" or "policy makers" are considered necessarily very different and distinct from "civil servants" or "careerists." This distinction, thought of as crucial to democratic control of the bureaucracy and referred to as the "politics-administration dichotomy" in the public administration literature, does perform a very necessary function, that of underscoring the need for modern government to be blessed by both direct accountability to the voters and a permanent staff that can attend to the technical details of administration. Clearly, both elected leadership and career expertise are needed, and my proposal in no way denies this dual requirement of democratic administration.

My argument makes, rather, three other, closely related points. First, at the top echelons of executive power, the politicians and careerists have far more in common in terms of their duties and responsibilities than a sharply demarcated politics-administration dichotomy readily admits. They both bear great leadership responsibilities, they both perform "public" jobs, they both feel the political heat intensely, they both make big and lasting executive decisions. Second, in the American political culture at least, both groups of leaders interact constantly. They continuously share influence and inevitably become interdependent on one another. The sharp contrast between minister and career civil servant that is found in Britain and its constitutional offshoots and in many European countries does not prevail in the United States.

My third point is that top elected and career executives can be viewed as joined together by membership in a common profession, the "political profession," which possesses certain distinctive characteristics to be spelled out in detail below. These common characteristics should be recognized for what they are and promoted to ever greater levels of attainment. Although I certainly do not argue that all present top executives are "pros," some are; and if we are to attain Professor Ransone's goal of responsible but decisive government, many "hams" now in power should become "pros."

This line of argument will, of course, require us to reconsider several well-accepted notions. One is the idea that professionalism is an inherently bad concept that fosters narrowness or parochialism in government. Some observers instinctively react negatively to the concept, on grounds that professionalism promotes the interests of particular groups, such as schoolteachers or social workers, rather than those of the whole. Let me quickly state that the concept being advanced here does not advocate narrow, self-serving action, but instead calls for broad intellectual scope, tolerance for the views of others, and a pursuit of the common weal. When, in the context of the argument being advanced here, executives are ideological, self-righteous, and self-serving, they are not political professionals but political amateurs unworthy of their calling.

Similarly, the notion that politics or politicians are inherently evil is likewise rejected. This view is, of course, patently naive, but it nonetheless forms the underlying basis for many governmental reforms in our history, including early civil service laws. The "reform" viewpoint I am advocating here—and it is reformist in the sense that political professionalism is advanced as an ideal as well as a reality—does not seek to "clean" the politics out of government, but rather to demand that everyone holding high power in government subscribe to a politics that serves the public interest.

The naive notion that career public administrators do not engage in politics is also implicitly rejected. All informed observers of government know that top careerists such as bureau chiefs and city managers do and must exert political influence and make policy. We have known this as a truism in the field of public administration since at least the works of Paul Appleby. Nonetheless, a lingering image of administrators as technicians remains in the public mind. My position also rejects the cynical view that activist administrators are perforce irresponsible program entrepreneurs or empire builders. Administrators who are political professionals may seek to build programs, but not for their own sake.

What Is a Profession?

Some twenty-one definitions of *profession* are found in the sociological literature, according to Geoffrey Millerson (1964:8). These tend to fall into two general camps: specific attributes of what were once called the "learned" professions (theology, law, and medicine), and the substantive content of a more generic definition of professionalism.

The first definition is exemplified by a list of nine characteristics of a profession proposed by William J. Haga (1974:3–10). To him, a profession is an occupation that involves service to the public; requires long training; embraces a code of ethics; publishes learned journals to upgrade practice; forms voluntary associations; uses examinations as a barrier to entry; does not permit advertising of services; employs symbolic costumes such as black robes or white coats; and limits practice to licensed or certified practitioners. Haga also regards the professions as having the capacity of denouement, that is, the ability to rectify profound human crises by means of esoteric problem-solving interventions. The doctor, for example, miraculously cures the sick, the lawyer releases the jailed, and the priest secures forgiveness for the sinful.

Bernard Barber (1963:15–34) offers a shorter list of traits whose conceptual nature permits a broader view of professionalism. These are a high degree of generalized and systematic knowledge, extending beyond the knowledge realms of the original learned professions; primary orientation to the community interest rather than to individual self-interest; a high degree of self-control of professional standards and conduct through internalized ethics and voluntary associations; and a system of rewards that portrays the work achieved as important unto itself, rather than as a means to self-gain. In view of this last feature, remuneration is not by monetary riches alone but also by prestige and honor.

The public administration literature has long struggled with the issue of whether trained civil servants can be regarded as professionals. The usual motivation for pursuing this line of thinking is a degree of inferiority felt by U.S. public administrators in our society's pecking order. As a result, "public management" is portrayed as a profession, and governmental specialists such as environmentalists, foresters, and public health workers are seen in this light. This viewpoint usually relies on the more generic definitions of professionalism to bring such occupations under the honored mantle. Hal G. Rainey and Robert W. Rackoff, in commenting on this issue (1982:319–35), are careful to show that though public employees can be considered professionals, their professionalism is not identical to that of lawyers and doctors. Their knowledge base certainly calls for informed expertise, these commentators say, but tends not to be as content-specific as law and medicine. Administrators value autonomy, even though they recognize that external regulation and oversight are essential and desirable. Finally, their commitment is to the organization as well as to the profession, and their service ethic is more focused on service through government than at the personal plane.

Concern in the public administration literature for the professional status of career public servants and public sector executives does not extend to political appointees or elected officials. This is because the field's principal conceptual duality is politics versus administration, not professionalism versus amateurism. The implied reluctance to embrace politicians is illustrated by the way the field treats Don K. Price's (1965) famous "four estates," the scientists, professionals, administrators, and politicians. The estates of the professionals and the administrators are merging, many public administration writers argue, while those of the scientists and politicians remain segregated. Richard C. Kearney and Chandan Sinha (1988:571–79) state that one advantage of such professionalized administration is that it permits administrators to facilitate cooperation and understanding between the Scientists and the Politicians. It also promotes bureaucratic responsibility and counters the common ailments of bureaucracy, they say. To make my own position clear, the amalgamation inherent in the concept of political professionalism extends only to the top executive levels of government. Political professionals do not include all or even most civil servants, or for that matter legislators, judges, and executives in the private sector.

Traits of the Political Professional

Let us now turn to the model of political professionalism being advanced here. It is, as I have said, both descriptive of what I regard as the best of executive leadership and prescriptive in the sense of constituting a proposed ideal for such leadership. The model comprises four elements: a competence for mobilizing and wielding power; a capacity for synthesizing diverse objectives, interests, and operational elements; a willingness to exercise discretion yet do so within constraints; and possession of a service ethos.

The Competence for Power

A foremost trait of the political professional is the competence to mobilize and wield political power. Competence for power is essential for executive leadership. Any characterization of power-consciousness as darkly evil or inappropriately "Machiavellian" works against a proper understanding of the crucial role of the political professional in society. Although acquiring and using power can have unpleasant aspects from the vantage point of the serene and tranquil life, its "nastiness" derives from the tough emotional qualities required of power holders, not an inherent immorality. After all, doing good in society often requires ugly high-stakes power transactions—or "dirty hands," as we sometimes say.

Holding political power is what permits the political professional to accomplish what he or she is uniquely qualified for—the reshaping of communities and societies on a collective basis. Only the political professional can define policy agendas, shape agency missions, develop policy objectives, forge administrative programs, garner public resources, create political alliances, fight determined enemies, and win powerful friends. These activities together permit the political professional to perform the societal denouement comparable to the doctor's curing of the sick and the attorney's releasing of the jailed. The miraculous intervention in this instance is the ability to secure authoritative action by government on a large enough scale to make actual impacts on the population of a city, county, state, or nation. In short, it is the ability to use government to make a difference in the lives of large numbers of people, an ability possessed by no one else. The campaigning politician can only promise; the sitting legislator can only prescribe, urge, and inquire; the media commentator can only bemoan and criticize; the judge can only deal with disputes brought before the court; the intellectual can only ponder and lament. Only the senior executive in government, the person actually in command of resources and acting in the name of legitimate authority, can *act*.

Action at the level of high politics requires a particular competence. The actor must be capable of doing things that most people would not enjoy, such as being under fire, being required to take controversial stands, being forced to attack others, and being subjected to the merciless gaze of the media. One must have an "appetite" for conflict and controversy and possess the "guts" for infighting and struggle. Yet, paradoxically, one must at the same time have a penchant for inspiring others, persuading skeptics, and building trust. Personal charisma as well as an instinct for battle is necessary, a difficult psychological combination to achieve. In addition to all this, the top player in the game of high politics must possess several complementary qualities, such as extraordinary energy, great stamina, unusual powers of concentration, and, above all, supreme self-confidence.

This competence for power is required by both the elected and the top career executive, I am arguing; *both* are engaged in the tough and dramatic dimensions of the public policy drama.

Conversely, both elected and career executives can be amateurs in the corridors of power. In fact, tendencies in this direction can be seen in each role. Campaigning politicians acquire "street smarts" in running campaigns and negotiating deals, but upon winning the election they discover that campaign skills alone are not enough to govern. The ability to translate promises and deals into practical programs and dynamic organizational leadership requires the quite different skills of the political professional. For their part, appointed administrators may be accustomed from their earlier career experiences to writing hard-edged memos and dominating small-group meetings but not engaging in high-intensity conflict over whose ox will be gored. Even if we are not accustomed to such notions of amateurism, we intuitively hesitate to elect an inexperienced candidate to high office or allow the management technician to get over his head in the upper echelons of political power.

A competence for power also requires an understanding that wielding power over other human beings is a privilege, not a right. Amateurism in this regard is illustrated by the periodic scandals in which governing power is misused, such as Watergate and the Iran-Contra affair. Here the problem is not a lack of ability to stride confidently down the corridors of executive power, but a lack of realization that the opportunity to do so derives from one's possession of this heady opportunity only by virtue of occupying, temporarily, a public office. Only the amateur uses power competence to break laws, undermine the Constitution, enrich oneself, or perpetuate the regime. The seeking of power for its own sake is the antithesis of political professionalism. Unfortunately, many technical experts at the power game, such as the Gordon Liddys and Oliver Norths of our world, are unable to rise to a professional plane in politics because of the base motivations that draw them to the pinnacles of executive power in the first place.

A Capacity for Synthesis

A second trait of the political professional is the capacity to synthesize diverse views and operational elements. This capacity is the equivalent for the political professional of the generalized and systematic knowledge possessed by the technical professional. One does not gain this knowledge from formal educational programs or articles in learned journals, however, and it cannot be tested in licensing examinations or certification procedures. Instead it is acquired from experience at lower levels of political responsibility, as in the municipal political machine or the middle layers of a government agency. Also, quite probably, one must have a personal propensity for what is required, for not everyone can learn to synthesize.

The mobilization of diverse resources is probably the most succinct way to characterize the executive act of synthesizing. This expression does not adequately capture all that is involved, however, for what is required is not merely the gathering together of the necessary people, funds, equipment, and facilities to undertake an administrative task, although this too is essential. Beyond such economic synthesizing is what might be thought of as political synthesizing, that is, the reconstituting of unfocused demands so as to support a focused vision.

When the executive leader wishes to achieve a true policy impact, he or she invariably faces a cacophony of diverse voices as to what should be done. Orchestrating that background sound into an intelligible political composition is the challenge. The problem is twofold, requiring both a response to the political environment and manipulation of that environment. On one hand, the background voices must be heard and answered, by accepting policy ideas from outside and listening to the demands of external groups. Plans must then be forged that at least respond to, if not comply with, the overall aims of constituents. On the other hand, the inner voice of the political professional must be heard, a vision for the future that the professional wants to impose on the issue at hand. The resultant synthesis thus absorbs others' views while reshaping personal views into a larger vision.

This bilateral process requires delicate balance and finesse. The professional may have to obscure the differences among competing interests, for example, by using vague terminology and symbolic phrases that mean different things to different people. The professional must also be able to convince competing constituents that only by standing on common ground will any progress be possible. The professional will then need to lead a developed coalition in an articulate and forceful manner so that the new reality of the symbolic goal takes on the intended stamp and desired momentum.

Again, diverse, almost contradictory, personal characteristics are required. The political professional must lead but also follow. The political professional must "have a dream" but also avoid doctrinal rigidity. The political professional must be far ahead of everyone else in the parade yet intimately familiar with the petty worries and narrow perspectives of those in the rear ranks of the procession. A splendid example of such professionalism can be seen in the work of General George C. Marshall, as he led the process of adopting a plan to reconstruct Europe after the war. Marshall freely entertained diverse views on what should be done and consulted widely with political leaders throughout the government. Yet he was also careful to build a consensus that embodied his own expectations of the bold action that was required. Marshall then pursued his course forcefully and methodically, without breast-beating or demanding personal recognition as the "savior" of Europe.

The political amateur, by contrast, lacks this delicate balance between leading and following. The amateur may follow but not lead. This happens when the technician lacks a larger vision or the politician is obsessed with satisfying all groups so as to be reelected. In both instances apathy and drift result. Another pattern of this form of amateurism is to insist on articulating goals very precisely so they can be rationally measured, thus destroying opportunities for obfuscation and amalgamation. This is the disease of "managerialism" in government. The opposite kind of amateurism is to lead but not follow. This amateur is ideologically driven and hence unable to adjust to external influences or enter flexibly into negotiations over policy; the anticommunism of J. Edgar Hoover exemplifies. Finally, the leader may be amateurish in the sense of becoming so ego-involved in policy that departure from personal plans becomes intolerable; General Douglas MacArthur's conduct in the Korean War is illustrative here.

Discretion Responsibly Exercised

The political professional must balance not just leadership and followership but also autonomy and accountability. One of the characteristics of a profession is a substantial degree of collective self-governance through standard setting and regulation of conduct by the profession itself. Within this framework of self-regulation the practicing professional operates alone but is held accountable to a code of ethics adopted by the professional association and to examining boards and review panels established by the association.

In the political profession an analogous situation prevails. Here the professional possesses great autonomy, not by virtue of esoteric knowledge and thus unquestioned judgment (except by peers) but by virtue of holding a high government office where discretion is conferred by statute or constitutional provision. The president "shall take care that the laws be faithfully executed." The typical department head in federal or state government is granted sweeping discretion to act "in the public interest" or "in all instances where deemed appropriate." The mayor of a city possesses extensive police powers to maintain order and protect the general welfare.

The check on this autonomy, the counterpart in government to regulation by codes and boards in the learned professions, is our system of what is sometimes loosely called checks and balances. In a constitutional system of government the governors are themselves governed—by competing branches of government, by bills of rights, and by the laws they themselves enact. The equivalent to a code of ethics for the political profession is the texts of federal and state constitutions and statutes and the judicial decisions deriving from them. Their licensing boards are in effect the election boards, legislative bodies, and city councils, which authorize entry to office. The counterpart to the profession's conduct-review panels is the system of auditors, prosecutors, inspectors general, legislative committees, grand juries, and courts that are available to overturn excessive or arbitrary action.

In this system, then, the political professional is held accountable in the exercise of professional discretion by governmental peers, just as are other professionals. The professional association is the government itself, including the corpus of authority in which it operates. Just as in the case of the practicing lawyer or doctor, entrance into the political profession and its association is voluntary, in that one does not need to seek high office. But once in that office, one is subject to its constraints as well as its privileges.

It is in this light that we can understand why some political behavior, even by politicians considered masters of their craft, is so jarring to our sensibilities, so amateurish. Richard Nixon acted unprofessionally when he authorized the Watergate break-in, and Ronald Reagan did so when he permitted overtures to Iran for an arms-hostage exchange. Conversely, when William Ruckelshaus restored a legally mandated order to a demoralized Environmental Protection Agency and Frank Carlucci returned an out-of-control National Security Council to its proper statutory function, these achievements were acts of professionalism in the deepest sense.

A Public Service Ethos

The final feature of political professionalism is service to the public, not merely to oneself. Service to the community is considered to be an essential component of professionalism. The doctor, the nurse, the attorney, and the clergyman practice so as to render service to others. The primary goal of their work is not to make money or acquire authority for its own sake but to perform their remarkable denouements. We all get irritated by physicians who drive expensive sports cars and attorneys who collect exorbitant fees. The underlying reason for this irritation is that their reason for being is not to earn profits, as is the case with the investor or businessman, but to help others.

The concept of a public service ethos fits well into notions of professionalism associated with the civil service. As Rainey and Rackoff note, the bureaucrat's service is not rendered as an individual but by means of organized government. In recent years several attempts have been made to elevate the concept of civil servant from neutral implementor of laws to an independent contributor to the public interest. Robert Reich has urged (1985:1617–41) that the public administrator become a fomenter and facilitator of constructive deliberation over public policy. Gary Wamsley and associates (1990) have called for the acceptance and encouragement of an "agency perspective" which regards public bureaucracies as unique repositories of special knowledge, institutional history, and consensus on concepts of the public interest. I have taken the position (1990:96–113) that public administration fosters, within the polity, important public-regarding values such as concern for ultimate effects, a futurist orientation, an interest in equity, and a willingness to place new items on the public agenda.

Although a public service ethos by career public servants is clearly a desirable and, in part, realizable goal, this does not mean that we should dismiss elected politicians as not imbued with such an ethos. We tend to "bash" our politicians as well as our bureaucrats, and perhaps a logical next step in reemphasizing idealism in government is to reconsider the value of democratically elected officeholders. Our mayors, governors, and presidents and their personal staffs and cronies—as controversial and partisan as they are—perform work that is important unto itself, just as is the case with other professionals. Since they must win election and reelection, we tend to see such figures as merely self-centered attention grabbers, insincerely pandering votes and cravenly seeking campaign contributions. Yet most politicians know that to achieve any lasting fame, which is the ultimate in ego gratification, one must leave behind things that will be remembered. The great reputations of President Harry Truman, Governor Nelson Rockefeller, and Mayor Richard Daley endure precisely because, in addition to the endless power plays and backroom wheeling and dealing, they left monuments of positive policy accomplishment. It is the amateur politicians, those who use their office to serve only themselves rather than their publics, whom we quickly forget.

The real issue is not, however, whether a public service ethos permeates more fully the career civil service or the ranks of elected officials. Such an ethos is present in both and absent in both. The point is that in all executive leaders a purely monetary incentive or power obsession alone is an inappropriate standard. Minimizing such political amateurism must always be a concern of the highest order in the democratic polity.

Conclusions

I have argued that to achieve Professor Ransone's objective of responsible yet effective governance, we must advance a set of values on the part of executive leaders which can be regarded as a higher form of public service. This political professionalism embraces a competence for power, a capacity for synthesis, the exercise of responsible discretion, and the embrace of a service ethos. These traits can be shown to be tied closely to concepts of professionalism usually reserved for the learned or expert professions. I am, in short, calling for an extension of the meaning of professionalism to include not only trained specialists but also our high-ranking government executives. Moreover, I am including in this category not merely high-level career administrators but elected executives who come to their jobs through partisan politics rather than formal training.

I take this position for three reasons. First, elected and appointed executives do essentially the same things at the highest levels of government—they manipulate the levers of power via policy, resources, agendas, images, and plans. The politics-administration dichotomy has tended to obscure our understanding of this point. Second, these executives do these things together, in an intimate and interdependent union. Policy is thrashed out, programs are governed, and agencies are led by the two working closely in concert, not in separate compartments. Third, we can elevate our expectations for both kinds of executive by the same rhetorical and normative device, a concept of political professionalism. Despite public cynicism about government, current executive leaders of both types already exhibit such professionalism in sufficient degree to make the category usable as a framework for evaluation. Prominent discussion and application of the concept in American governance circles as we near the new century would constitute a splendid and lasting memorial to Coleman B. Ransone, Jr.

2 FINDING THE PUBLIC IN PUBLIC ADMINISTRATION

H. George Frederickson

Public administration is our profession and our discipline. We assume that the term *public administration* is descriptive of the concepts and theories that make up our discipline and the decisions and actions that form our craft. Should we not, therefore, also seek to assure that both of the words in the phrase are fully defined and generally understood? The word *administration* is the subject of extended study, analysis, and discourse. Theories of administration abound, and approaches to improving or making administration better are everywhere to be found.

The word *public* is, however, another matter. There are few developed definitions of "the public" or descriptions of how that public should or ought to connect with our discipline and our work. There are some surrogates for the word *public* that are in common usage and about which there is some study and theorizing, such as citizenship, the public interest, the common good, and the common will. Our primary approach to understanding the public is conveniently to assume that government is akin to the public; yet we know that they are not only different entities but they are in fact starkly different. The subject of government, of course, is the platform upon which political science rests and about which we have fully developed theories and extensive experiences and practice.

In public administration we ordinarily use government as the surrogate for public; yet we continue to use the phrase *public administration*, rather than *government administration* or *government management*, as the primary descriptor of thought and practice in our field. But we have virtually no elaboration of the word *public* in public administration.

If we persist in using the term *public administration*, and if we believe it to be a fair descriptor of both thought and practice, would it not be important to describe and define the public more fully and develop the beginnings of perspectives or concepts of the public in public administration?

This essay explores the meaning of *public* in *public administration*.

The Meaning of *Public*

The classic meaning of *public* derives from two sources or roots. The first is the Greek word *pubes*, which meant maturity. Maturity in the Greek sense means both physical and emotional or intellectual maturity, to include moving from selfish concerns or personal self-interest to seeing beyond oneself to understand the interests of others. It implies an ability to understand the consequences of individual actions on others. *Public*, as the derivative, means moving to an adult state, understanding the relationship between the individual and other individuals, and an ability to see the connections (Palmer, 1981:18).

The second root for *public* is the Greek word *koinon*, from which the English word *common* is derived. The Greek word *koinon* derives from a second Greek word, *Komois*, meaning to care with. Common and caring with both imply the importance of relationships.

Maturity and seeing beyond oneself seem to indicate that the word *public* can be both a thing, as in the case of a public decision, and a capacity, as in the case of the ability to function publicly, to relate to others, to understand the connection between one's actions and the effects of those actions on others (Mathews, 1984:122–23). Adding the words *common* and *caring with* to *maturity* makes the case even stronger that *public* means not only working with others but looking out for others.

David Mathews reminds us that the Greeks had "two words for private. One word described an individual who was able to understand only his or her own perspective. The Greek word for that kind of private person has become our word 'idiot.' The other term for 'private' though is not at all negative, but quite the contrary. The second word derives from the Greek 'oikos,' for family or household. There is nothing wrong in attending to one's own household, nor does it preclude attending to public matters" (Mathews, 1984:122–23).

It appears that the origin of the English word *private* likely means to be deprived of a public life. Parker Palmer pointedly reminds us that "the private status that we so value in our day, the life on which we lavish such energy and attention, was once regarded as a state of deprivation" (1981:18).

The Greeks conceived of the public as a political community—the polis—in which all citizens (in the Greek case adult males and nonslaves) participated. The political community was to establish standards and practices and to support, promulgate, and enforce those standards. The standards were for the greater good. Loyalty from the citizen to the city-state was significant as was the city-state's responsibility to protect and "care with" the citizen.

The modern English usage of the word *public* has both retained and lost some of its original meaning. We refer to the public to mean all the people in a society, without distinguishing among them. A public school is open to all and is thought of as a place where the common knowledge of the people is passed along. The public press is available to all, as is the public library. The English "pub," or public house, has always been a gathering place for the entire community. And we continue to use the phrase *a public figure*, which means a person whose responsibilities and, therefore, much of his or her life are visible to all.

Much has been lost. *Public* has come to be a synonym for politics or government. We study and practice politics and government but seem unable, as Mathews puts it, to deal with the concept of public "as an independent idea" (1984:122–23). The word *public* is often regarded as so vague or ambiguous as not to be useful. *Public* implies to some a challenge to individualism, to others opposition to private business, and to others an inclination to collectivism. It gets worse because to many *public* means the trivial, the ordinary, the vulgar, and the masses (Mathews, 1984:122–23). And when the public is tied to other words such as *the public good* or *the public interest*, it is often seen as so idealistic or romantic as to be impractical or useless.

What happened? The philosophy of the utilitarians has replaced the Greek perspective on the public and has dominated political thinking and governmental practice for 150 years. Collective attempts to find and govern toward a greater good were replaced by individual calculations of pleasure or pain, personal utility or costs and benefits. The purpose of government was reduced to private well-being. We are to determine well-being, pleasure, or utility by consequences or results, preferably by bureaucratic, technological, or scientific means. There is no public, only the sum of atomistic individuals. And there is no public interest, except in summing up the aggregate of private interests (Leys, 1952:13–32).

Utilitarian philosophy has been influential in or compatible with the development of the market model in economics—we can judge consequences or results by the technology of the market—and the public choice perspective on public administration. The faith in science and technology to answer questions and solve problems is wholly compatible with utilitarian philosophy and with much of early public administration. Positivism in law, which argues that law is the command of the sovereign rather than a codification of the public will or the greater good, is utilitarian. Finally, attempts to apply "decision-theoretic" analysis to achieve efficiency and economy to public agencies are utilitarian.

Utilitarian philosophy has contributed to significant improvement in public administration because of its emphasis on efficiency, economy, bureaucracy, and technology, but it also contributed to the loss of an ennobling concept of the public. Certainly the present use of *public* has moved away from the classic meanings. But both the classic and contemporary meanings of the word are filled with implications for the theory and practice of public administration.

Contrasting Perspectives on the Public

Public administration does not focus on the definition or meaning of the word *public*, yet in twentieth-century philosophy the concept of public has received extensive treatment. Those who have studied the public in this century, led by John Dewey (1954), are generally agreed that the public seems to be lost.

Often in philosophical discussion the issue turns on the distinction between those things that are private and those that are public. The most common breakdown, of course, is human actions that affect only one person as against many, or the distinction between self-regarding and other-regarding actions. Dewey says that when the actions of some affect the welfare of others, the act "acquires a public capacity." The public, to Dewey, is not fixed but is created and recreated, depending on actions and interactions between people. The public was lost because it seemed unable or unwilling to organize itself into a political community for the general protection of common interests. The public is lost because it cannot *act* as a public (Dewey, 1954).

Walter Lippmann, by contrast, indicates that the public is lost because there is an absence of a public *philosophy*. To him the assertion of individual rights has resulted in a loss of a sense of public responsibility for the effects of individual decisions. In the absence of a public philosophy, we consider the consequences of most human actions as strictly private, without anyone taking responsibility for public acts (Lippmann, 1955).

Richard Sennett, in *The Fall of Public Man* (1977), agrees with the earlier views and states boldly that there is no recognizable public realm left. Our preoccupation with our private selves causes us to understand everything that occurs outside of the self as a reflection of that self rather than distinct from the self. All actions are defined depending on how they affect each individual. With such a perspective, there can be no public as distinct or separate from the aggregation of individuals. Under such circumstances, how can an individual or an aggregate of individuals share responsibility for collective action?

It is puzzling that the word *public* has come to have such a narrow meaning in our time. We think of the public as pertaining to government and having to do with voting and the conduct of elected officials. We do, of course, think of the public policies as those that are made by a representative government that are binding on all. Parker Palmer asks, "Why has this word—which should evoke common bond in a diverse people—taken on such a narrow political meaning? I suspect the answer lies in an assumption which pervades the political thought of our society, the assumption that only through the processes of government can a public be created, and only through legislative enactment can the many become one" (1984:47).

Political theory, heavily influenced by utilitarian philosophy, seems primarily concerned with self-interest. Public thus emerges primarily as a means to umpire and control the diversity of self-interest. Palmer notes: "The task of government is to provide a framework of rules and penalties within which a community can be constructed out of the convergence of self-interest, with those interests which do not fit being deflected or simply denied. In this stream of political theory, the public has been reduced to an arena in which individuals compete for the most they can get, with the government as the referee" (1984:47). Palmer argues that this image of the public holds no promise for an authentic public life. It provides no vision or unity and does not lead toward community.

The agreement that there is a loss of the public seems not to be associated with liberalism or conservatism. Indeed, both liberal and conservative philosophers seem to agree on this point, perhaps for the wrong reasons. The liberal philosopher William Sullivan, in his treatise *Reconstructing Public Philosophy*, suggests that the modern premises of liberalism, coming to us from Thomas Hobbes, John Locke, Adam Smith, and John Stuart Mill, foster excessive individualism, anti-public spirit, competition among warring self-interest groups: they militate against a sense of the common good. He continues: "Conceiving human beings as exclusively self-regarding, liberal philosophies use human association as a kind of necessary evil, and politics as an arena in which the clashes of individual and group interests can be more or less civilly accommodated. As a philosophy of government and social life, liberalism exalts both the supremacy of private self-interest and the development of institutional means for pursuing those interests. In its extreme form, this philosophy denies meaning and value to even the notion of common purpose, or politics in its classic sense" (Sullivan, 1982:xii).

The well-known conservative George Will has a similar critique. He suggests that politics has been reduced from a concern for civic virtue to a concern with power and order. He is especially concerned with the social contract because it locates "the origins of government in an agreement between the rational, self-interested but pre-civic persons. They are motivated to associate neither by neighborliness (affection) nor political allegiance (shared political philosophy), but only by anxiety about their physical safety and the security of their property" (Will, 1983:30). These views are strong, but they are probably not altogether right. The so-called liberal origins of the concept of public, while fostering self-interest and individualism, also have resulted in significant social gains in justice, freedom, and equality (Murchland, 1983:15).

Most philosophical commentators agree that the public is lost. Why?

David Mathews suggests that when one distinguishes between the public as practice and the public as an idea, one finds that the unavailability of the former is owing to the unavailability of the latter (1984:122–23). Because we are unable to practice or exercise the concept of public as action or capacity, we find it impossible to develop a very compelling idea of the public, let alone a theory.

Modern political scientists, particularly the so-called behavioralists or logical positivists, have studied the "public interest." They believe that the public manifests itself through groups or organizations and other complex aggregations. Whatever way the public acts or behaves is assumed to be the public interest. If there is a popular will, it is the sum of the interaction of the interest groups legitimized through the governmental and political process (Schubert, 1960).

Despite the negative views of both philosophers and empiricists, the fact that we have a functioning society certainly means that there is a public spirit at work. Many forms of public life exist to channel individual and collective energy to a common or public set of purposes. To be sure, self-interest, individualism, greed, and consumerism everywhere flourish, but the polity functions. The question for all, and especially for those who think and practice public administration, is how really to be *public* administration rather than just government administration.

Framing the Public in Public Administration

Ordinarily, public administrators are government employees. It should be no surprise, then, that our theory and practice revolve around the functioning of the city, the county, the state, and the nation-state. Should we assume that the city, the county, the state, and the nation-state set the intellectual agenda for public administration? Is there a role for public administration beyond or in addition to the functioning of particular governments? What are our responsibilities to the public we ultimately serve?

The characteristics of modern society mitigate against the effectiveness of modern public administration. Orion White reminds us that there has been a sharp decline in the ability of the public at large or of public agencies to act authoritatively. He suggests that "it is the American bias against authority that has led us to accept a reified image of the human being as merely a satisfaction-seeking organism. We now virtually have what we say we have wanted: a society without authority, where each of us is marching to his own drummer, held together as a society mostly by our technical infrastructure" (1981:216). No wonder it is not easy to run a government these days. White suggests a solution, which is to transcend the traditional concept of citizenship, "which allows us to talk mostly about what we need in order to feel good—and find a format for communicating about our mutual realization and development. Such a point of orientation will allow us to be more open to the establishment of authoritative social institutions. Where the use of authority is seen as being aimed toward the positive maturation and development of people rather than a way to referee the competition for the resources required for the gratification of needs, it is more acceptable" (1981:218).

Not only does the culture mitigate against the development of a fuller conception of the public, but public administration itself is part of the problem. One of the dominant themes in contemporary public administration theory is the so-called public choice perspective derived primarily from utilitarian logic. Public choice theorists and practitioners favor the lowest common denominator of government agencies and the designing of government agencies for the purpose of setting the rules by which people compete for costs and benefits. Such a perspective holds the marvelous convenience of calculation and is a haven for the methodologist. The analyst with an Apple computer, software, and data can calculate the best possible distribution of resources. Public administration is thereby reduced to "decision making," the calculation of distribution following minimal levels of political acceptance. Such a public administration is bereft of a purpose beyond the routine and ordinary day-to-day application of our job descriptions (which, incidentally, we do very well).

A common theme in modern public administration is the differences between so-called public and private administration. The drastic narrowing of both the idea and the practice of public has resulted in a concomitant growth in what is currently defined as private and/or business. Originally, the corporation was a public enterprise chartered by a government agency to engage in commerce, but for the common good. Robert N. Bellah and his colleagues remind us:

> Reasserting the idea that incorporation is a concession of public authority to a private group *in return for* service to the public good, with effective public

---

accountability, would change what is now called the "social responsibility of the corporation" from its present status, where it is often a kind of public relations whipped cream decorating the corporate pudding, to a constructive social element in the corporation itself. This, in turn, would involve a fundamental alteration in the role and training of the manager. Management would become a profession in the older sense of the word, involving not merely standards of technical competence, but standards of public obligation that could at moments of conflict override obligations to the corporate employer. (1985:290)

Following this conception of corporate responsibility, it could plausibly be argued that both government employees *and* corporate employees are public administrators (Bozeman, 1987). Public employees are directly engaged in the managing of government functions such as police and fire or the conduct of national defense, the so-called indivisible public goods. By contrast, corporate employees are engaged in the provision of goods or services for sale to the public. To what extent, then, can members of the public assert that they have as much say in the manner in which goods and services are prepared and presented for sale as they have in the organization and delivery of government services?

There can be little doubt that the old and simple distinctions between public and private no longer pertain. For example, the Defense Department and the National Aeronautics and Space Administration (NASA) make agreements with major defense and space contractors. Which is more directly in the public service, the contracting officer at NASA, or the persons responsible for delivering safe, reliable, and fairly priced defense and space equipment? Are they not both responsible to and for the public?

We have so narrowed the definition of public and the public interest as to leave the public with what appears to be great freedom and a laissez-faire business environment. Have we actually broadened the definition of private so greatly as to leave the public without an effective and authoritative way to express common interests above and beyond buying a Ford rather than a Chevrolet? Narrowing the definition of public has resulted in approaches to business administration education that are under heavy criticism for being shortsighted, noncompetitive, and preoccupied with the appearance of progress through merger as against real growth and development.

The critique of public administration thought and practice is probably not very much better. We pursue efficiency, economy, order, and predictability. Like good utilitarians, we tend to have a high regard for moral ambiguity. We stress operating efficiency, procedural due process, protecting the boundaries and longevity of each bureau and agency, and reducing all big issues to questions of means and short-run benefits. We avoid policy discussions that focus on purposeful long-range ends. Louis Gawthrop refers to this as an ethics of civility. In this ethics we function under the rule of law, not of men, based on written codes and standards. We seek to do good by avoiding doing evil. Because we cannot define good, it is easier to find what is wrong and try to fix it. We assume that through the detailed specification of what is wrong, public officials can be counted on to do what is right. Gawthrop argues that this results in a static, dry, barren desert of mediocrity and unresponsiveness. Civility, he suggests, will be failed reform (1984:138–45).

Gawthrop offers a creative ethic designed not for a static but for a dynamic world. Because the world is dynamic, sociopolitical reality cannot be found in objectivity. It can only be found in relating. "The objective situation must always be replaced by the evolving situation, which depends extensively on the cumulative development of progressive experience." The real reality, according to Gawthrop, "is in the relating, in the activity between the subject and the object in any behavioral interaction. Yet reality emerges from the endless evolving of these relatings, and indeed relating emergent component situations, which also might be called the evolving situation" (1984:146).

Gawthrop is describing the public both as an idea and as capacity. The capacity here is the structured pattern of interaction between public administrators, interest groups, elected officials, and the public at large to find the evolving and changing public will. In this pattern there is no escape from responsibility. And there is no collective responsibility. Only individual responsibility will do. We cannot be absolved because we work for government, and we should not be absolved because we work for corporations. All are, to some degree, public officials.

With this conception of public administration, we include not only our obligations as government employees to carry out the laws of the land efficiently and effectively but constantly to exercise an ethic of concern for our neighbors and for those who are "furthest away."

In our culture, thinking has never been as important as doing. Experience has always been more important than theory as a guide to action. Bernard Murchland puts it well: "Experience rather than theory generates the controlling metaphors of public life: process, plurality, experiment, growth. That is why the native philosophy of this country is the radical empiricism of the pragmatist. . . . The point is not that ideas are not important; but rather that if they are not realized in experience, they're not deemed much good" (1984:14).

There is a great danger in this pragmatism, this learning by doing and by experience. It can result in anti-intellectualism and thoughtless action which cripple the ability of the public to function. Murchland points out that "to feel the truth before we know it is to run the risk that we may only feel it and never know it. . . . The fact is, practice soon becomes inchoate without theory, and the pragmatists themselves are always out of balance between the respective claims of each." It is for this reason that theory is often as important as action. Theory holds the promise of grounding practice in legitimizing concepts, visions, and ideas. "Public in the strong sense means knowing as well as doing; above all it means knowing in common what we can never know alone" (1984:14).

One of the unfortunate effects of narrowing the idea and practice of public to the functioning of government has to do with careerism. If, in our education for and practice of public administration, we define ourselves as only government employees, we prepare the seedbed for careerism and individualism. When public administration is defined more broadly to include the effective operation of government agencies coupled with a structured pattern of interaction with the public to improve the common good, it heightens the potential that persons will choose a life in public administration for reasons other than pure ambition.

To many in public administration, the public seems too large and abstract to identify with and respond to. Indeed, utilitarianism was partially a response to urbanization and industrialization, arguing that public affairs were too large and complex to operate like the Greek city-state. For this reason we have been slow to develop a cogent theory of the public. There may be an emergent theory, and if so it would likely include conceptions of the company of strangers, overcoming problems of space and public relations, the validity of impersonal relations, and developing the contemporary public of interdependency.

The Company of Strangers

Can there be an authentic public life in the company of strangers? Parker Palmer notes that "the vision and reality of community come when people have direct experience of each other, experience of mutuality, interdependence, unmediated by governmental sanctions and codes. The vision and reality of community come when people have a rich array of opportunities to interact in public, interactions which draw out and encourage the human impulse toward life together" (1984:49). We find this interaction most commonly in public streets, where strangers in pursuit of private interests meet. The public can be the encounter of strangers occupying the same territory, the same human community, impressed with the need to acknowledge that fact and the impulse to get along. Parks, squares, cafes, museums, and galleries are settings for public life, where strangers can meet, spend time in each other's presence, and share common interests. These interactions are multiplied by rallies, forums, hearings, and debates, where more formal interaction among strangers can occur. The neighborhood is an important setting for public life. Increasingly voluntary associations provide a setting in which strangers come together. The point is that a healthy public life involves continual interaction with other persons moving in and out of one another's lives in an endless panorama of meeting, interacting, leaving, and meeting again. This public life is as authentic and valid a form of human experience and is as able to authenticate common and shared beliefs as other forms of human interaction. It is the public as both an idea and a capacity.

The Problem of Space and Public Relations

The nature of public life can be determined by the quality of space in which the human interaction can occur. Where neighborhoods are separate from commerce and both are separate from parks or squares, it is more difficult to see the structured interaction of strangers. The need for strangers to leave their neighborhoods of rows and rows of homes and the long hallways of offices to find the modern equivalent of the town square or the public place is clear. Our present arrangements of space do not enhance the public life. Two developments hold some hope: the rising importance of the architecture of public places and contemporary television and communication. We see in the works of Charles Goodsell, the author of our first chapter, the significance of the architecture of public meeting places (Goodsell, 1988). The purposeful design of public places to do more than facilitate commerce, to enable meeting in forums, councils, assemblies, schools, and other public ways, is critical to a reemergence of an effective public. Televising public meetings helps, especially if it includes audio feedback for questions and comments from the "distant" public. The preoccupation with automobiles and the tendency of persons to move via automobile from work to tract homes and return lessens the opportunity for the company of strangers.

The Validity of Impersonal Relations

The public life is also partly determined by the psychology and mind-set of our time. Richard Sennett makes this important point:

> The reigning belief today is that closeness between persons is a moral good. The reigning aspiration today is to develop individual personality through experiences of closeness and warmth with others. The reigning myth today is that the evils of society can all be understood as the evils of impersonality, alienation, and coldness. The sum of these three is an ideology of intimacy:

social relationships of all kinds are real, believable, and authentic the closer they approach the inner psychological concerns of each person. This ideology transmutes political categories into psychological categories. This ideology of intimacy defines humanitarian spirit of a society without gods; warmth is our god. (1977:259)

The problem comes from an impression that all meaningful relationships must have closeness and warmth. Although closeness and warmth are critical to one's private life, "the problem arises when we impose the norm of intimacy on public life. For in the public realm, where most relations are necessarily distant and impersonal, the demand for closeness and warmth distorts and eventually destroys the potential for public experience" (Palmer, 1984:47).

From this we become preoccupied with the personal characteristics of others, their style and appearance. The personal characteristics of persons in public life rather than their intellect, views on the issues, or capacity to affect the general good become the dominant interest. In addition, when we personalize the public life, we begin to fear that if we were to enter public ranks, our own private lives would become subject to scrutiny and criticism. This fear causes us to withdraw. Parker Palmer points out: "Historically, Americans have worried about the incursion of public powers in the private realm. But now we see that there is also a problem when the psychology of private relations is forced upon the public sphere. . . . We must learn to accept and appreciate the fact that public life is fundamentally impersonal. . . . To receive full benefit from public life, one must realize that impersonal relations have a validity of their own" (Palmer, 1984:47).

The Contemporary Public of Interdependency

The world is too complex to attempt to reconstruct the Greek city-state, but it is possible to rebuild the public through an understanding of human interdependence. The atomic age, the era of international air and water pollution, famine, and the increasingly global nature of the economy all indicate our international interdependence. Homelessness, drug addiction, poor schools, and highway gridlock inform us of our local interdependence. Through technology we now know directly the horrors of war and famine. We may be reconstructing the public because the excesses of utilitarianism have created an increasingly strong sense of interdependence. The company of strangers is now both local and global. We experience the circumstances of unknown others and join them, usually in brief or sporadic ways, in a public. A general sense of the public good, at least in our collective responsibility to each other in basic humanity—nutrition, shelter, education, work, protection—seems at least possible in the emerging global village. Interdependency may drive us into each other's arms.

Conclusions

We see here the beginnings of a conception of the public that can serve public administration. Such a conception would include recognition that the public is not the same as government. The public lives independently of government, and government is only one of its manifestations. We also know that there is public as an idea and public as a capacity. By reducing public to government we limit the capacity of people to be public. As an idea, the public is all persons relating together for public as against personal or family purposes. The public as capacity implies an informed, active ability to work together for the general good. In many cases, but not always, that will be through government. Voluntary organizations, not-for-profit organizations, and corporations are all manifestations of the public. It follows, then, that public accountability or responsibility is in enabling the citizens to set agreed-upon community standards and goals and in working in the public's behalf to achieve those goals. Public responsibility and accountability are expected of both public and corporate administrators. One cannot hide behind "private" or "business" to escape responsibility to the public. Nor can one hide behind the organization, government, or business. Public responsibility is not collective but is individual.

Within the framework of the Constitution and regime values, public administrators have a responsibility to structure relations between organizations and the public so as to foster the development of an evolving conception, on the part of both the organizations and the public, of the common good. Elections, legislative decisions, executive policy, court decisions, and the continual pattern of interaction between public officials and the public are expressions of public preferences. We must nurture and protect these forms of interaction so as to come as close as possible to an evolving creation of the public and therefore an evolving definition of the public will.

3 PUBLIC LEADERSHIP: A DEVELOPMENTAL PERSPECTIVE

Robert B. Denhardt and Kevin Prelgovisk

Many commentators have argued that improved leadership in modern society is essential for us successfully to meet the challenges of the late twentieth and early twenty-first centuries. Seymour Lipset and William Schneider report, for example, that their review of public opinion data reveals "a widespread loss of faith in the leadership of business, government, labor, and other private and public institutions" (1983:3). Moreover, as Terrence R. Mitchell and William G. Scott (1987:445–52) argue, this lack of confidence is not a generalized discontent with working conditions, social institutions, or life in general. Rather, it is specifically *leadership* that is being called into question.

We would argue, however, that the problem is not merely related to those in *formal* positions of power but a failure of leadership throughout society. As John Gardner has stated: "In this country, leadership is dispersed among all the various segments of society and down through all levels, and the system simply won't work as it should unless large numbers of people throughout society are prepared to take leaderlike action to make things work at their level" (1987:2). What seems required is an improved capacity for human beings to exert leadership, whether in the family, the work group, the community, or the nation-state. Such an effort will require that we first understand clearly the nature of the leadership process, then develop programs of training and education that will stimulate in individuals those qualities that underlie effective leadership. Such programs, however, should take into account the changing nature of leadership in our society. In this chapter, therefore, we will introduce a particular approach to leadership—what we call public leadership—and suggest that this approach is increasingly appropriate, indeed necessary in the modern age. We will then examine the range of skills associated with public leadership.

Recent Studies of Leadership Behavior

One of the many difficulties in understanding leadership is that the term is used in so many different ways. For this reason, we must preface our discussion of public leadership with some commentary on the breadth of recent studies in leadership behavior. One of the continuing themes in such studies has been the attempt to identify the leadership traits and personal characteristics of well-known leaders, an effort limited because history provides examples of leaders who exhibited vastly different personal qualities and yet achieved major accomplishments, or feats of "leadership." From Alexander the Great to John Kennedy to Mohandas Gandhi, those who have "led" appear to have done so by a variety of means. Some are thought to have been able to lead by virtue of the personal power, or perhaps because of the charisma surrounding their personas; others because of the moral vision they were able to elicit from their followers.

One contemporary version of the effort to identify traits or personal characteristics suited to leadership, Fred E. Fiedler's Cognitive Resource Theory, appears to have encountered similar difficulties. Intuitively, it would seem that the most effective group leaders would be the ones who are the most intelligent, the most competent, and the most experienced in the nature of the work being done. And, indeed, Fiedler concludes that "more intelligent leaders develop better plans, decisions and action strategies than do less intelligent leaders; that is, plans and decisions more likely to result in effective performance" (Fiedler and Garcia, 1987:201). Other studies, however, have shown "the rather counterintuitive finding that measures of leader intelligence show only a low positive correlation with the performance of their groups or organizations" (e.g., Fiedler and Garcia, 1987:201). Having persons with high competence, intelligence, and experience in leadership positions does not necessarily assure effective group performance. There are some conditions under which even intelligent group leaders may be ineffectual.

Other work explores the character of the individual personality. For example, Abraham Zaleznik believes that "managers and leaders differ fundamentally in their world views. The dimensions for assessing these differences include managers' and leaders' orientation toward their goals, their work, their human relations, and their selves" (1977:70). He speculates that leaders may have a different psychological grounding than managers: "Managers and leaders have different attitudes toward their goals, careers, relations with others, and themselves . . . leaders are of a psychologically different type than managers" (1977:67). The consequences of these differences for groups are that managers and leaders may lead groups to produce entirely different outcomes. Managers help groups decide how to do something whereas leaders help groups decide what to do, if indeed they need to do anything at all. As Warren Bennis and Burt Nanus comment, "Managers do things right. Leaders do the right thing" (1985:21).

Leadership is often examined in terms of traits or attributes of personality, but we would argue that leadership is a much larger concept that cannot be isolated from the social process of the group, the organization, or the nation-state. For this reason, we feel that attempts at understanding leadership that focus on the lives, traits, and personalities of individual leaders apart from the group process are destined to fail. Such studies may be useful in helping an individual gain an understanding of what leadership is about, but they cannot by themselves provide adequate preparation for the leadership function.

We find more compelling the work of James MacGregor Burns, who recognizes the interactive nature of leadership by referring to its transactional, transformational, and moral aspects (1978:448–54). In his view, the terms *transactional* and *transformational* describe two basic leadership types. The transactional leader essentially uses a bargaining process to maintain control: politicians who exchange votes for jobs illustrate this kind of "transaction." Transformational leadership seeks to exploit the needs of potential followers by addressing their motivation and higher needs. A third leadership type, moral leadership, "emerges from, and always returns to, the fundamental wants and needs, aspirations, and values of the followers" (Burns, 1978:448). Though similar to transformational leadership in its attempt to reach the basic needs and aspirations of its followers, moral leadership adds the dimension of social action and change.

Burns argues that the legacy of the leadership process is a changed society, of which "the most lasting tangible act of leadership is the creation of an institution—a nation, a social movement, a political party, a bureaucracy— that continues to exert moral leadership and foster needed change long after creative leaders are gone" (1978:454). He believes this ongoing change is perpetuated by morally purposeful individuals who elevate both followers and themselves in the process. Burns recognizes that the creation of an institution enhances the opportunity for continued social change, but he understands that it does not necessarily guarantee such change. He suggests that "the most lasting and pervasive leadership of all is intangible and non-institutional. It is the leadership of influence fostered by ideas embodied in social or religious or artistic movements, in books, in great seminal documents in the memory of lives greatly lived." It is the perpetuation of those great ideas, "in the hope of enabling more lives to be greatly lived" at all levels of society, that leads us to focus on the relationship between leadership and development (1978:455).

Leadership and Social Development

Our interpretation of leadership draws from previous efforts but also differs in important ways. Conceptually, we view leadership as a transcendent process that goes beyond mere personalities or positions. As we see it, leaders are characterized by their ability to understand the underlying motives and desires of a group and connect them to the social context in which the group can act. For this reason, we argue that leadership is better understood as an aspect of social development than of power and that when leadership is conceived in this way, new possibilities for public leadership become available at all levels of society.

In this position we differ slightly from Burns, who, like many others, defines leadership as an aspect of power. Power, for Burns, "is exercised when potential power wielders, motivated to achieve certain goals of their own, marshal in their power base resources . . . that enable them to influence the behavior of respondents by activating [their] motives" (1978:18). In Burns's view, leadership is exercised when the intentions of leaders and followers meet.

In contrast, we view leadership not as a mode of power but rather as an aspect of social development, especially the development of groups and organizations. (Although we focus here on the leadership function in groups and organizations, we feel that the lessons we draw from these levels of interaction apply as well to many other levels.) Social development, as we use the term, implies increased autonomy, flexibility, and creativity on the part of the group or organization in dealing with its environment. It implies not only the capacity of the group or organization to grow in conventional terms (resources, size, complexity) but to satisfy the intentions of its members to provide an improved structure of shared meaning.

The term *leadership* focuses on the role of the individual in stimulating social development. We define leadership as the character of the relationship between an individual and a group or organization that stimulates or releases some latent energy within the group so that those involved more clearly understand their own needs, desires, interests, and potentialities and begin to work toward their fulfillment. Leadership refers to the actions of an individual, but always in relation to the group or organization.

There are several reasons why we prefer to think of leadership as an aspect of social development rather than of power. First, power, in most of its forms, involves control, the capacity of one person or group to get another person or group to do something it would not otherwise do. Moreover, power is typically held by an individual (or vested in a position) and is exercised so as to achieve an established purpose, typically one defined as being in the interest of the power holder. For this reason, to define leadership in terms of power tends to confuse leadership with the instrumental pursuit of established interests. Though many whom we call leaders exercise power, it is not their exercise of power that makes them leaders. When leadership is present, something occurs in the dynamics of the group or organization that leads to change, but that something need not be an exertion of power. Indeed, as we will see, efforts by the leader to control the group are ultimately destructive of leadership. When the direction of the group or organization is selected through a developmental process—one that gives priority to the needs and desires of the members of the group rather than the power wielder, leadership is much more likely to be enduring. It is also more likely to enhance the opportunities of individuals in the group or organization: in this way it becomes emancipatory rather than restrictive. In addition, leadership, as an aspect of social development, is clearly a process rather than a position; here leadership is regarded as a group function rather than as a capacity of an individual or a position, a point that is not always clear in other treatments of leadership. Burns, for example, occasionally refers to leadership as a process, but his orientation toward power inevitably focuses his attention on power holders or positions of power. Leadership becomes associated with individuals or positions rather than being seen as something that shifts from person to person and from group to group over time.

In turn, a view of leadership as a process enables us to examine leadership at all levels of society. Leaders are not only the potential power wielders, the governors, the presidents, the kings and queens. Rather, leadership is a pervasive phenomenon, occurring in families, in work groups, in businesses, and at all levels of government, society, and culture. Anyone can be a leader, whether for a moment, a few days, weeks, or years. The argument in behalf of improved leadership, as we understand it, should not be limited to improved rulership. Rather, it is our feeling that both individuals and society generally would benefit from improvements in leadership at all levels.

Public Leadership

Leadership can occur in several ways. Typically, leadership involves helping the members of a group become aware of a new direction in which they wish to move, in most cases a new direction that already is present in their subconscious. Leadership, in this sense, is a capacity of the group, a resource that lies within the group and must be activated for the group to fill its potential. Leadership taps and reshapes the consciousness of the group; it provides an integrated vision that many share. Leadership may be likened to the action of light on a dormant seed: it allows the development and emergence of something that lay already complete yet unrealized. It affects the members of a group in a way that is psychologically compelling: they feel drawn to action and to pursuit of a new vision. Acts of leadership, then, are acts that express a new direction, but a direction that is determined by the emerging interests of all the group's members. It follows that without some degree of reciprocity, the acts of a potential leader will be seen as isolated from the group, a process that could eventually lead to the destruction of the relationship.

One way such damage occurs is through the potential leader's concern for personal rather than group interests. A leader pursuing his or her own interests—perhaps even exercising rigid control—may be successful for a time, for even under these circumstances the latent energy of the group or organization may be tapped and leadership may occur. If the leader's interests happen to coincide with those of the group, or if members happen to recognize an interest of their own reflected in the actions of the leader, change may come about. Typically, however, as soon as the leader's interests or purposes begin to diverge from those of the group, the leader begins to close communications and to resort to the exercise of power rather than leadership. Under such circumstances, leadership soon dissolves into control, as so often happens in large organizations. Traditional modes of hierarchical organization are paradigmatic examples of the dissolution of leadership into institutionalized mechanisms for control. We will refer to the exercise of power and persuasion within such structures as private management.

Leadership, however, need not pursue private or predetermined interests in a closed manner. Instead, leadership can develop through an open and evolving process in which the values and interests of all members of the group are equally valued. Such public leadership involves a reciprocal relationship through which members of a group or organization express in word and/or in deed the shared interests of those involved in the relationship, interests that are established through an open and visible process. Public leadership pursues interests publicly defined (in an open and evolving relationship between two or more individuals) and is therefore expressive rather than instrumental.

Both private management and public leadership are concerned with moving the group or organization in new directions, but they differ significantly in the way they go about it. Private leadership typically involves a specific person holding the formal position of leader and assumes a commitment to established purposes, often merely those of the power holder. Specifically, the person designated the leader of a group or organization is expected to come up with good ideas about the direction the group should take, decide on a course of action or a goal to be accomplished, and exert his or her influence or control in motivating the group in that direction. Public leadership, by contrast, focuses attention on other matters. Specifically, public leadership is exercised by one who helps the group or organization understand its needs and its potential, integrates and articulates the group's vision, and acts as the "trigger" or stimulus for group action. Since public leadership involves a reciprocal relationship through which choices are made concerning the future directions of a group or organization, public leadership inevitably involves ethics and morals.

Public leadership does not simply mean leadership in government, but rather in all situations involving a mutual determination of direction and action. Denhardt (1984) has described public organizations as those characterized by ambiguity of purpose, multiple decision centers, and processes open to public view. A similar characterization could be applied to many other situations, including the relations between and among individuals, the operations of small groups, or even the actions of a nation-state. Whenever there are situations in which goals or purposes are unresolved, when those goals and the actions undertaken in their pursuit require broad participation, and when all these activities must be undertaken openly, public leadership is appropriate and necessary.

We believe that there is an increasing need in our society for public leadership. Modern society has been correctly described as highly turbulent, subject to sudden and dramatic shifts; highly interdependent, requiring cooperation across many sectors; and very much in need of creative and integrative solutions to the problems that face us. Under such conditions, ambiguity will increasingly be a hallmark of decision making and the involvement (rather than the control) of many individuals in group decisions will be necessary. Warren Bennis writes: "Leadership . . . will become an increasingly intricate process of multilateral brokerage, including consistencies both within and without the organization. More and more decisions will be public decisions; that is, the people that they affect will insist on being heard" (1983:16).

Harlan Cleveland (1985) similarly argues that the advent of plentiful and cheap information is changing the very nature of control in hierarchical organizations—indeed, it is undermining hierarchy throughout society. Because information cannot easily be bottled up, especially in the age of microcomputers and telecommunications, it is difficult, if not impossible, to prevent its dissemination. And because those who understand the value of information are becoming more and more prevalent in our information-rich society, the structure of decision-making groups must, by necessity, change. With more universal access to an understanding of information, leadership becomes even less a function of the power associated with controlling a scarce resource. Instead, the leader will be the one who is able to elicit purposeful group action based on shared information, that is, the one who asserts public leadership. The possibility for control is diminished, but the opportunity for leadership, as we define it, is enhanced.

Leadership and the Developmental Process

If leadership is viewed as a process of social development, then the preparation of people throughout society for leadership must also be viewed in a dual perspective—as closely related to the process of maturation and the growth of self-esteem. This point has been demonstrated in recent examinations of curricula and instruction in business and public administration studies that have suggested that the primary mode of teaching in schools of management, one focusing on the transmission of disciplinary-based cognitive knowledge, has not well equipped students in the areas of leadership and social responsibility.

Although the critiques mentioned here do not refer directly to programs in leadership education (though they would certainly embrace some such programs), several important lessons can be drawn from this critique and applied to leadership education more generally. Most important is the argument that cognitive knowledge alone is insufficient to prepare someone to assume a position of leadership or to exert leadership in a group situation. On the surface, the point is fairly straightforward—simply knowing *about* leadership does not make one an effective leader (just as knowing *about* communication docs not make one an effective communicator). But it is clear that a significant component of leadership education today seeks primarily a cognitive understanding of leadership. For example, some programs require students to read biographies of great leaders. Others require that they read major studies of leadership (including many of those cited in this chapter). The point is not that such practices are ineffective but that they are limited in their ability to prepare persons for active leadership.

Think for a moment of the way people acquire proficiency in other skill-based areas such as art or music or sports. Merely reading a book about golf will not make a person a good golfer. Although the book can provide a foundation for learning the game, developing real skill in golf requires sustained practice. The same is, of course, true of art or music. Cognitive knowledge can provide a foundation for action, but it cannot assure the effectiveness of one's action.

To some extent, schools of business and public administration have acknowledged this important lesson and have begun to design courses that involve students in practicing their interpersonal skills, either through cases, simulations, or internships. Programs in leadership education have been even more interested in developing such activities. For example, the Center for Reflective Leadership, part of the Humphrey Institute at the University of Minnesota, places great emphasis on participants' engaging in community activities that project from the classroom into the real world.

But beyond the acquisition of cognitive knowledge and the development of behavioral or interpersonal skills, something else is required for effective action. Going back to the sports analogy, even after hours on the practice range, the golfer may find that on the course, under conditions of great complexity and the stress of competition, shots that once seemed easy are extremely difficult. Similarly, the manager or leader who knows what to do and who has performed correctly on other occasions may find that under the conditions of uncertainty, complexity, and stress (those conditions we associate with the real world), actions may be difficult. For example, any modern manager knows the importance of extensive involvement and consultation before making major organizational changes. Yet time and again, people fail to consult and fail to involve, and as a result they encounter great difficulties.

This suggests that beyond acquiring cognitive knowledge and developing specific behavioral and interpersonal skills, potential managers and leaders must develop a certain psychological grounding that will enable them to act successfully under conditions of uncertainty, complexity, and stress. These skills involve self-understanding and self-confidence, but they reduce most clearly to self-esteem. For managers and leaders to resist the temptation to deviate from what they know to be correct, they must have a strong sense of self and a capacity to withstand the pressures of risk taking.

Based on work in development psychology, Denhardt has described these three sets of skills as follows:

> One's *cognitive knowledge* consists of one's store of information about the world, one's awareness and one's judgment. One's *interpersonal or behavioral skills* are those culturally specified and culturally approved ways of interacting that we employ in our normal exchanges with others. These include such standard patterns of behavior as communicating, negotiating, or engaging in relationships of power and authority. Finally, one's *intrapersonal or action skills* are those capabilities that both orient and enable intentional action, those that allow us to act with integrity and consistency in any given situation. (1987:127)

The two themes examined above, private management and public leadership, require many similar skills and capabilities on the part of the potential leader. But there are differences as well. We may consider the similarities and differences in the two approaches to leadership by looking at

Table 3.1. Skills Required for Various Leadership Modes

Sets of Skills	Private Management	Both Modes of Leadership	Public Leadership
Knowledge	Objective knowledge of the group or organization	Knowledge of the environment	Subjective knowledge of the group or organization
Interpersonal skills	How to use power and influence in pursuit of goals	Communication negotiation	Consultative and integrative skills
Intrapersonal skills	Rational and analytic	Self-confidence and self-esteem	Intuitive capacity for ambiguity and risk

the knowledge, interpersonal skills (behavioral skills), and intrapersonal skills (action skills) required for success under each mode (see Table 3.1).

Both modes require knowledge of the environment. Yet private management requires objective knowledge of the group and its capabilities, whereas public leadership requires subjective knowledge of the group and its aspirations. The former requires objective observation; the latter requires empathetic understanding.

Both require behavioral skills in communication and negotiation, but private management requires the ability to construct a strategic vision of the organization and skill in using power and influence in pursuit of that vision. Public leadership requires strong consultative skills (encouraging people to express their ideas and listening carefully to what they say) and the ability to integrate many differing but complementary ideas.

Both require self-esteem, self-confidence, and the ability to handle stress, but private management requires strong reasoning capabilities, whereas public leadership requires strong intuitive capabilities. Moreover, public leadership requires special skills in dealing with uncertainty and ambiguity and in accepting the risks associated with delegation. The public leader does not have the security of a position or office to hold on to and therefore needs an especially strong sense of self.

Successful leadership, therefore, requires knowledge and interpersonal skills, and it requires a heightened sense of self. Most of all, leadership requires self-reflection and self-critique, the prerequisites to building self-esteem. Bennis comments: "The task of the leader is to lead, and to lead others he must first of all know himself" (1976:200).

Education and Public Leadership

The development of the capacity for leadership is far more demanding than simply acquiring knowledge or developing specific behavioral skills. Such a perspective is clear in Cleveland's "core curriculum" for training people for leadership:

> Education in integrative brainwork—the capacity to synthesize for the solution of real-world problems the analytical methods and insights of conventional academic disciplines. Education about social goals, public purposes, the costs and benefits of openness, and the ethics of citizenship.
> A capacity for self-analysis—through the study of ethnic heritage, religion and philosophy, art and literature, the achievement of some fluency in answering the question Who am I? Some practice in real-world negotiation, in the psychology of consultation, and in the nature of leadership in the knowledge environment. A global perspective and an attitude of personal responsibility for the general outcome—passports to citizenship in an interdependent world. (1985:200)

The nature and range of the skills we have suggested as appropriate for public leadership clearly cannot be learned within a one- or two-year postgraduate course of instruction. Indeed, many will find that, as Burns suggested, the skills have, to some degree, to be learned by virtue of one's life experiences. Burns suggested that though leadership may be taught, it can be truly learned only as part of a total, lifelong process. He describes this process as

> not merely the importing of "facts" or the teaching of skills, indispensable though they are; it is the total teaching and learning process operating in homes, schools, gangs, temples, churches, garages, streets, armies, corporations, bars, and unions, conducted by both teachers and learners engaging with the total environment, involving influence over persons' selves and their opportunities, not simply their minds. . . . Ultimately education and leadership shade into each other to become almost inseparable, but only when both are defined as the reciprocal raising of levels of motivation rather than indoctrination or coercion. (1978:448)

In Burns's view, leadership education is a process in which teachers and students work together to seek truth and to motivate one another. This process involves the development of moral values and, presumably, assists the student in reaching higher stages of moral reasoning and development. Similarly, Cleveland's focus is on the self and the integration of the self into an increasingly complex world. In this view, the individual is best prepared for participation and leadership by an education that focuses on the synthesis of information, the integration of information for public—even global—purposes, and the practical application of that integration as evidenced by action. This model adds to Burns's ideas of leadership by the combination of the study of "great ideas" with the capacity for self-analysis and self-reflection. Although Cleveland's observation that we are in the twilight of hierarchy may be somewhat premature—indeed, for much of the world it is high noon—his notion of the development and integration of the self through a new curriculum for leadership is timely.

The vicarious experience of leadership by studying lives that have been greatly lived is an important component of leadership development. Yet probably even more important, education for public leadership can prepare individuals for leadership at all levels by enabling them first to know themselves better. Through interaction with fellow students and faculty and through personal reflection, students may gain a greater understanding of their own strengths and weaknesses. This period of education may be understood as a kind of personal sabbatical in which, besides gaining cognitive knowledge, students are free to explore new ways of interacting with others. Moreover, developing the skills needed to achieve consensus—practicing leadership—can be done in a relatively nonthreatening environment through participation in group processes. In this way the skills of public leadership can be practiced and refined. But most important is the opportunity for personal growth, the exploration and development of oneself, and one's capacity for public leadership.

We believe that some of those whose lives are greatly lived are able to offer public leadership because of well-developed interpersonal *and* intrapersonal skills. In turn, these are often the individuals who, by the depth of their understanding and by their own broad and varied personal experiences, are able to inspire others to greater heights. For the potential leader, we can only recommend the seeking out of quality in one's life experience. The benefits derived from travel, widespread reading, discussion with others, and actually doing things—a fully participatory involvement with life— will enhance the individual's perspective of the world and capacity to act. In this way the public leader may transcend the mere management of public values and instead help to refine those values through a simultaneous renewal of self and through undertaking acts of public leadership.

4 POLITICAL STRATEGY FOR THE POSTMODERN PRESIDENCY

Ryan J. Barilleaux

On the occasion of inaugurating a new president, the nation witnesses an event that has remained essentially the same since 1789. Each chief executive recites the same simple oath and then takes over the White House. An address and a parade usually accompany the ceremony. The whole event emphasizes continuity and the endurance of the American system.

This image is doubly deceptive. First, the office of president has not remained static but has undergone tremendous change since it was occupied by George Washington. Second, although the fundamental act of transferring power is the same as always, the powers transferred in a contemporary inauguration are somewhat different from those of times past. More important, the transfer of presidential power is now far more complex than reciting an oath. Although the occasion has special constitutional significance, it is but the climax of a larger process of transition from one administration to the next. The new president has wrestled with the problem of deploying the presidency at least since early November, and it will be some months before whatever passes for normalcy at the White House begins to take hold.

Every president confronts the staggering obligations involved in the metamorphosis from candidate to officeholder, but in our time a new chief executive must adapt to changes that are still only poorly understood. For the presidency of the late twentieth century is distinctive: it is not merely a continuation of the modern presidency created by Franklin Roosevelt but is so different as to warrant a new label. The past few years have seen the rise of a postmodern presidency as the office has undergone changes and adjustments in reaction to events and trends of the times. Although the contemporary presidency is not completely different from what came before, it has changed enough to demand that we take note of the transformation and its consequences.

One of the most important consequences involves a new president's transition to power. If they are to have any chance of succeeding at the job, new incumbents must understand the altered shape of the office and its demands. In short, they need a strategy for coping with the postmodern presidency.

The Shape of the Postmodern Presidency

In the past quarter of a century, the United States has experienced a series of significant social, cultural, and political changes. These shifts have transformed American politics: the New Left of the 1960s arose and then gave way to the New Right of the 1980s; the old political coalitions have been replaced by a "new two-party system" (Cavanaugh and Sundquist, 1985); reforms in the 1970s created a "new Congress" (Mann and Ornstein, 1981); the policy shifts and big deficits of the Reagan years marked a "new direction in American politics" (Chubb and Peterson, 1985); and some analysts have even suggested that the nation has seen the rise of a "new American political system" (King, 1978). In short, the politics of late twentieth-century America is different from what preceded it.

Likewise, the upheavals of recent years have affected the presidency. Recent decades witnessed the rise and fall of an "imperial" presidency under Lyndon Johnson and Richard Nixon, followed by a "postimperial" presidency under Gerald Ford and Jimmy Carter. Presidential power was revived under Ronald Reagan, a revival that has been carried on, albeit in a somewhat different way, by George Bush. Were these shifts merely superficial, or were more fundamental changes taking place?

The answer appears to be that the presidency has changed (Barilleaux, 1988; Greenstein, 1988:321; Rose, 1988). Ronald Reagan was the first postmodern president, but not because he alone created that position. Rather, he consolidated changes that had been building for years, adding his own innovations, and the result was a revised presidential institution. In 1989, George Bush entered an office that is substantively different from the one John Kennedy and Richard Nixon assumed in their own times.

It is not easy to make out the shape of the postmodern presidency, however, because of the incumbent. Since the presidency is such a personalized office, it is difficult to separate the office from the occupant of the moment. There is the rub. But it is not impossible because the specific aspects of each president can be excised to reveal the current shape of the office. For example, Reagan's skills as the "great communicator," his particular brand of conservative ideology, and his detached approach to management were features of the officeholder rather than the office. Similarly, George Bush's style of telephone diplomacy is idiosyncratic rather than institutional. Once such characteristics are removed, six distinguishing features of the postmodern presidency emerge: the revival of presidential prerogative power, governing through public politics, the president's general secretariat, vicarious policy making, the president as chief whip in Congress, and the new vice-presidency.

The Revival of Presidential Prerogative Power

Presidential prerogative power took a beating in the 1970s, with Congress's reaction to the Vietnam War, Richard Nixon's impoundment of funds appropriated by Congress, and Nixon's invoking of executive privilege to protect himself during Watergate. Laws were passed and actions taken to limit presidential power: the War Powers Resolution, the Case Act (requiring reporting of executive agreements), the Budget and Impoundment Act of 1974 (essentially preventing impoundment), the National Commitments Resolution (calling for all significant foreign policy commitments to be made in agreement with Congress), the legislated end to the Vietnam War, and prohibition of American involvement in the Angolan civil war.

Even in the face of this apparent decline of executive power, however, a revival of presidential prerogative was under way. Ronald Reagan certainly accelerated and expanded that renascence, but he did not begin it, for presidential prerogatives, some subtle and some blunt, have grown substantially over the last several years.

Foreign Policy Prerogatives

Despite attempts by Congress to restrain presidential power in foreign affairs, the chief executive's prerogatives are now stronger than ever. Three examples will demonstrate this point.

First, the War Powers Resolution, which was designed to limit the president's ability to commit American forces to combat without congressional approval (50 U.S.C. 1542, 1543, 1982), in practice has only required that presidents be cautious in their use of force. Presidents now must either keep American involvement brief (so as to avoid the law's sixty-day time limit) or seek congressional approval for extended action. In the 1975 *Mayaguez* incident, the 1980 raid on Tehran, the invasions of Grenada and Panama, the 1990 buildup of American forces in Saudi Arabia, and more than a dozen other relevant incidents since the law's passage, presidential military action was unrestrained by the War Powers Resolution (Franklin, 1987). In the case of President Reagan's dispatch of U.S. Marines to Beirut in 1983, a compromise was reached whereby Congress approved an extended (beyond sixty days) commitment of American forces, but the president never acknowledged the necessity of approval under the law (Fisher, 1985:317). In the case of the 1991 Persian Gulf war, President Bush made it clear that he would act whether or not Congress explicitly authorized him to do so. That fact encouraged legislators to support a popular and inevitable military operation. As long as presidents avoid a confrontation with Congress on a long-term commitment such as that in Vietnam, they are relatively free to act— provided they are subtle and choose their battles wisely. Indeed, the presidency has gained from the law: it now possesses a license to commit American troops to combat without congressional approval.

Similarly, attempts to restrain presidential autonomy through the 1961 Arms Control and Disarmament Act (22 U.S.C. 2573, 1982) and the 1972 Case Act (1 U.S.C. 112b, 1982) have created loopholes for imaginative presidential action in that area. These acts were constructed to restrict the president's ability to commit the United States to international agreements without the approval of Congress, yet from 1980 to 1986 the nation observed the limits of the unratified SALT II treaty. In short, Presidents Carter and Reagan took advantage of loopholes to achieve arms control by presidential fiat (Barilleaux, 1986; Barilleaux, 1988:10; Fisher, 1985:278–79).

The means for doing this was a device known as parallel unilateral policy declarations (PUPD). In January 1980, President Carter was forced by circumstances to ask the Senate to suspend consideration of his SALT II treaty. The United States and the Soviet Union then issued separate statements, identical in language, promising that each would abide by the treaty provided that the other side did likewise. Through this "nonagreement," the terms of the treaty were in force without ratification or even formal reporting to Congress. Later, Ronald Reagan continued American adherence to the treaty by the same device and even extended its life beyond its expiration date.

In the process, American arms control policy became in effect a presidential prerogative. Whereas until 1977 arms control was considered too important to be conducted without consideration by Congress (which as early as 1961 had demanded a role), by 1986 executive officials could speak of a future of arms control without agreements (Adelman, 1984–85). Of course, this implied arms control without congressional involvement.

Loopholes alone, however, were not the only source of revived prerogative power. In 1983, the Supreme Court's ruling in *INS* v. *Chadha* cast doubt that Congress would be able to order a president to halt military action through the War Powers Resolution because such "legislative vetoes" were unconstitutional (103 S.Ct. 2782; Fisher, 1985:313; U.S. Congress, House, Committee on Rules, 1984). In 1979, the Court had struck down Senator Barry Goldwater's challenge to President Carter's termination of the American defense treaty with Taiwan. The Court's ambiguous ruling in *Goldwater* v. *Carter* (444 U.S. 996, 1979) seemed to establish a new presidential prerogative to end treaties (Fisher, 1985:270–72).

Budgetary Prerogatives

Another important feature of the postmodern presidency is the new importance of budget policy making. Once centered in the departments and agencies and largely incremental in nature, executive budget making is now dominated by the White House. Indeed, it is best characterized as top-down budgeting: budget decision making is centered in the president and his Office of Management and Budget (OMB) director, who oversee executive branch units in their preparation of budget requests (McMurty, 1986:16–17; Heclo, 1984:262–70; Schick, 1984).

Presidents have long sought to acquire centralized power over budget preparation because budget requests reflect government priorities in the allocation of federal revenue. The more centralized is the system of executive budget making, the more potential a president has to put his stamp on policy. Efforts by presidents from Kennedy to Carter were generally unsuccessful, but more recent attempts have been more effective because President Reagan made budget cutting a top priority and improved computer technology helped the OMB acquire the necessary data to direct budget preparation. Through his first budget office director, David Stockman, Reagan was able to impose a top-down budgeting system on the traditional executive budget process. Under President Bush, this centralization has continued, with Budget Director Richard Darman using a two-track system of budget request preparation, control over executive-legislative budget "summits," and other devices to ensure White House dominance over executive budget making.

A second factor affecting the executive budget was the revision of the congressional budget process. In the 1974 Congressional Budget and Impoundment Act and the 1985 Balanced Budget Act, Congress centralized, rationalized, and disciplined its own budget procedures so as to exercise greater control over federal spending policy and compete with the presidency. As the newly formed congressional budget committees became the focus of legislative decision making on spending, the role of the OMB and thus the president in executive-legislative budget politicking was enhanced.

Administrative Clearance

The expansion of federal government activities in the twentieth century, particularly since the 1960s, has resulted in an explosion of administrative activities. Administrative rule making has become the most common form of federal legislative activity, far outstripping the lawmaking efforts of Congress. To cope with this rule making, the postmodern presidency now possesses the power to review and delay all rules proposed by executive agencies.

The process of administrative clearance, as this review is known, had its origins in the 1970s but was consolidated by President Reagan in Executive Orders 12,291 (1981) and 12,498 (1985). Through the OMB, particularly its Office of Information and Regulatory Affairs, Executive Order 12,291 requires that all proposed agency rules be reviewed and justified through cost-benefit analysis (Rosenberg, 1986; West and Cooper, 1985; Ball, 1984). Each year, the OMB reviews about twenty-five hundred federal regulations. Of these, 85 percent are approved without changes, 12 percent are approved with changes, and the rest are rejected. Significantly, however, the effect of the orders extends beyond acceptance or rejection: agency rule makers must now consider the OMB's powers and the president's views in their rule-making process. President Bush has maintained this power, and his successors will probably want to keep it as well.

Prerogative power is back. From military force and arms control to budgeting and regulation, the postmodern presidency possesses powers not held earlier in the twentieth century. These prerogatives do not guarantee a president success in achieving goals, but they give chief executives additional leverage and autonomy in their efforts to shape public policy.

Governing through Public Politics

Another feature of the postmodern presidency is its reliance on public politics for influencing the direction of policy. That reliance is a recent phenomenon, but an important one.

The presidency was not created necessarily to be an office of public leadership, and indeed part of the reasoning behind the Electoral College was to insulate the executive from public support. Yet it soon became such an office, at least from the time of Andrew Jackson's election. If not all presidents since then have been great popular leaders, it was not because the presidency was a remote institution.

The connection between presidents and the public intensified in the twentieth century, as the rise of mass society, expanded federal government activities, and new technology changed the nature of American politics. Indeed, responding to these changes, Presidents Nixon, Carter, and Reagan exhibited a tendency to govern through public politics. President Bush has done so as well, although by using televised press conferences (thirty-two in his first year and almost daily in the early stages of the Iraqi crisis) more than television addresses to get his message to the nation. This practice of "going public" involves presidential appeals to the American public for support for himself and his policies (Kernell, 1986).

Not only is the resort to public politics a common feature of the postmodern presidency, but public support for the president is a significant determinant of presidential influence in Congress (Edwards, 1980:86–100; Edwards, 1983:199–208). A popular president has more influence than an unpopular one. George Bush has been careful to protect his strong approval rating, and in 1989 his secretary of state suggested that the president could use that support to stare down his critics. Moreover, a president who is able to mobilize public support for his policies, as Ronald Reagan did most effectively on behalf of his first budget in 1981, can win important votes in Congress.

Of course, use of public politics does not guarantee success, but it has become a significant aspect of the contemporary presidency. It means not only that the chief executive's influence is more vulnerable to swings in public opinion but that presidential efforts to build popular support are also a major feature of the postmodern presidency. These efforts include protection and manipulation of the presidential image such as the careful staging of public appearances, "photo opportunities," and controlled press conferences. Postmodern presidents not only use public politics to govern but realize that the entire public face of the presidency affects their ability to do so.

The President's General Secretariat

The postmodern presidency has at its disposal a sort of general secretariat, a central staff that enables the chief executive to direct and supervise the work of the executive branch. This secretariat is better known as the Executive Office of the President (EOP), and in recent years it has developed into an important support staff for presidential government (Hart, 1987). Although the EOP has been a significant feature of the presidency ever since its creation under Franklin Roosevelt, the Executive Office occupies a much larger role in contemporary government than it did in earlier years. It is a powerful, bureaucratic, and politicized extension of the president (see Newland, 1984; Moe, 1985; U.S. Congress, House, Committee on Energy and Commerce, 1981). Its dominance can be seen through two important trends in national executive politics: the rise of the OMB and the institutionalization of the National Security Council (NSC) as a key agency in the foreign defense policy arena.

The reasons for the importance of the OMB revolve around the growing importance of budgetary issues in American government. As the budget has grown more and more to be the focus of policy decision making, the OMB's influence has increased. Thus a large role for the budget office was inevitable no matter who became president in 1980. But the election of Ronald Reagan, his battles with Congress, and the establishment of a long-term deficit problem for the nation ensured the OMB's significance in future policy making (see Peterson, 1985).

The OMB's influence extends beyond budgets. It has long operated a legislative clearance process, whereby its Legislative Reference Division coordinates, reviews, and clears hundreds of legislative proposals that emanate annually from executive agencies to Congress. The division also reviews agency reports to Congress and testimony on proposed laws and informs congressional committees of how pending legislation relates to the president's program. Finally, it advises the president on bills readied for his signature or veto. In short, legislative clearance is a major tool for presidential control of the executive branch.

Administrative clearance arose in the 1970s to complement legislative review. Because of the growing volume and significance of federal executive regulations, presidents since Richard Nixon have attempted to control rule making by administrative agencies. But supervisory power over rule making was held by the agencies themselves. That situation changed with initiation of the administrative clearance process, which has consolidated the OMB's dominion over the review process. Because the rise of administrative clearance has been a long-term process, and because it gives the president capacity to control the executive branch, this centralized review will likely continue to characterize the postmodern presidency.

The rise of the OMB is complemented by the institutionalization of the NSC. Through its staff and as a forum for policy coordination, the NSC now serves as an important component of the foreign and defense policy decision process. It enables the president to oversee all aspects of that process, maintain a presidential (as opposed to departmental) perspective on security issues, and balance the competing interests and contributions of the State and Defense departments (Destler, 1981). In the last five administrations, the NSC has also coordinated decision making in all areas of national security affairs. It has thus been institutionalized—its role has been secured and made permanent. Most of the value of the NSC appears to lie in the ability of the national security adviser and his staff to expose the president to the range of opinions and options relevant to his decisions. Future presidents will not ignore the NSC because they need its support.

The EOP is now big, bureaucratic, and powerful, but it has become so to assist the president. As a result, presidents need more help to operate and manage this general secretariat. Such control requires more formal organization and hierarchy of staff than some presidents have desired. Kennedy and Johnson could eschew formal structures and disparage bureaucracy in the White House, but Jimmy Carter was forced after emulating them to appoint a chief of staff (Kernell and Popkin, 1986). President Reagan never attempted to run the White House without such an aide, nor has President Bush. The necessity for a chief of staff is a fact of life in the postmodern presidency.

Vicarious Policy Making

The postmodern presidency makes policy not only through direct actions of the chief executive, the White House staff, and the OMB but also through the president's appointments to positions in the federal judiciary and independent regulatory commissions. Such influence is in effect vicarious policy making.

Vicarious policy making occurs when a president's influence is felt through the actions and decisions of his appointees, particularly those who have independent power to make authoritative governmental decisions. In such cases, the president either takes vicarious pleasure in seeing his appointees make policy as he would wish it to be made or experiences disappointment because someone he named to office has acted in a way contrary to his expectations. Recent presidents have seen both: President Nixon got what he expected when he named William Rehnquist to the Supreme Court, whereas Dwight Eisenhower regarded the appointment of Earl Warren as chief justice as one of his greatest mistakes.

The main point here is more a qualitative than a quantitative one. It is that a considerable portion of a president's impact on the governing of America lies in what his appointees do. Whether a president makes a few regulatory or judicial appointments or many, those choices will help to shape important policy decisions for years to come. Long after a president is gone, his influence may be felt through the work of his appointees, regardless of whether he would have agreed with them, because he put them in office. This fact has become even more significant in recent years as the policy-making power of courts and regulatory agencies has expanded (Agresto, 1984; Ball, 1984). A single vote on a commission or the Supreme

Court can shape a policy ruling that will have far-reaching effects, as the 1990 nomination of Judge David Souter to replace retired Justice William Brennan illustrated. One vote can affect rules governing abortions, requiring that a product be withdrawn from the market, mandating a higher interest rate, and a host of other significant and binding policy decisions.

The President as Chief Whip in Congress

If they are to succeed in their relations with Congress, postmodern presidents must do more than their predecessors had to do to develop their influence in that body. They must act in effect as the chief whip in Congress.

Whereas their predecessors could work with powerful committee "barons" and influential members to write laws, postmodern presidents find a very different situation. The open Congress of the late twentieth century is a place of much greater decentralization than the legislature of even two decades before. As a result of changes in rules and customs during the 1970s, the contemporary Congress is a place of fragmented power. Postmodern presidents must act as chief whip to build their own coalitions.

What must a president do to cope with the new Congress? Several points are clear. As Norman Ornstein has noted:

> To prevail these days, a president must first accept a cardinal premise: he will be required to know and to deal regularly with a much wider array of players in the process, members *and* staff. Such dealings require a congressional liaison staff that works to know not just who the members are, but what they like and dislike, who needs to be sweet-talked and who can be bullied, who will be satisfied with a special White House tour for constituents or an invitation to a state dinner and who will insist on a substantive concession. Knowing the members also means maintaining an active, ongoing intelligence operation to achieve early warning of who might introduce a surprise amendment or oppose a presidential initiative or be vulnerable at a given future moment to a particular presidential plea. (1983:204)

This scenario resembles the information and skills associated with a legislative whip. A president who is not willing to act as one runs a serious risk of failing with Congress. Jimmy Carter's early problems with Congress can be directly attributed to his misunderstanding of Ornstein's cardinal premise.

But the president cannot be chief whip alone. An effective legislative liaison staff must be available to provide information and do the head-counting and cajoling involved in building a coalition. The president and liaison staff must understand Congress and its operations if they are to make it work for them.

Moreover, the president must be willing and able to establish and communicate legislative priorities and to become involved in the process of lobbying Congress through bargaining and public politics. A president without clear priorities will, like Jimmy Carter, find the legislative process jammed: President Carter sent Congress a long list of proposals in 1977 but provided no sense of which were most important. As a result, action on all of them was stalled. President Bush has also encountered problems with Congress because he did not clearly articulate a legislative program in his first year. In contrast, Ronald Reagan's priorities were clear to legislators, and Congress acted on them. Having priorities does not guarantee success, but not having them effectively ensures failure.

The president cannot, however, announce priorities and then retire. Serving as chief whip requires being actively involved in politicking with Congress. Presidents must use the knowledge they have, the threats and favors at their disposal, and their own reputation and public standing to induce Congress to cooperate. More of the president's limited time than before must now be spent in "working" Congress: making phone calls, meeting with members, maintaining close relations with congressional leaders, and other related activities. Being the whip is a demanding job.

The New Vice-Presidency

The final characteristic of the postmodern presidency is the new vice-presidency. The past two decades have seen the transformation of the republic's second citizen from a minor political figure into an important presidential adviser (see Light, 1984).

In the wake of Watergate and Gerald Ford's accession to the presidency, followed by two "outsider" presidents in Washington, the vice-presidency has become a position that offers its incumbent an opportunity to be among the small circle of senior presidential aides and counselors. Recent vice-presidents, particularly Walter Mondale and George Bush, have demonstrated a potential for influence in an office that was long ridiculed for its unimportance. They have done so because the presidents they served were willing to allow them a larger role than their predecessors held. Moreover, since both Presidents Carter and Reagan were "outsiders" in Washington, their "insider" seconds provided useful information and connections to the centers of power in the capital.

As a result, the vice-president has become a useful adviser to the president, able to offer the benefit of knowledge of public issues, the policy process, and political strategy. Moreover, the vice-president's institutional resources for an activist role have been enhanced. Rockefeller, Mondale, and

Bush were guaranteed unlimited access to their president, and by using that privilege (not always granted in the past) wisely each was able to stay closely in touch with the daily business of the White House. The vice-president's staff has also increased; it now includes seventy or eighty professionals. Even Vice-President Dan Quayle, whom many observers assumed would be a throwback to the old vice-presidency, has used staff resources and the trend toward greater power in his office to build a larger role in the Bush White House. Quayle was even put in charge of the crisis-management team that dealt with a 1989 coup attempt against Philippine leader Corazon Aquino while President Bush was en route to the superpower summit at Malta.

This trend is significant for several reasons. First, the vice-presidency now provides better preparation for the top job than ever before, should an emergency accession occur. Second, since the new electoral politics that has developed in the last two decades has restored to outsiders a serious chance of capturing the White House, insider seconds will probably be valuable into the future. Third, the other developments that characterize the postmodern presidency contribute to a chief executive's need for an activist second. Not only must presidents be able to handle the various aspects of the job well, but they need a chief of staff to help keep up with their responsibilities. They can use the advice that the senior politician called the vice-president has to offer. The new vice-presidency is likely here to stay.

Taken together, these elements form the outline of the postmodern presidency. Many of these trends, such as the growth of the president's staff, have roots stretching back much earlier in the century, but in the past two decades the institution has changed in ways that separate it from the past. As a whole and as the sum of its parts, the postmodern presidency constitutes a new version of the nation's highest office. The consequences of this situation are many, but chief among them is that new presidents will be unable to lead unless they understand this new version and develop a strategy for dealing with it.

Advice to a New President

Presidential candidates are struggling to win an election and have precious little time to think about assuming office. Yet, as James Pfiffner (1988:156) has made clear, that is exactly what they must do so as to make the most of the campaigns they undertake.

All candidates have ideas about what they want to do if and when they reach the White House. That is their affair. But prospective presidents need help in forming a strategy to cope with the revised office they hope to assume. What follows, then, is a political strategy for dealing with the postmodern presidency.

Get Your House in Order First

Because the postmodern presidency includes a large and powerful general secretariat that is crucial to the functioning of the office, new presidents must face the problem of internal White House management before they can face their other responsibilities. If they do not do so, they will not be able to get on with the business of government.

Before assuming office, the prospective president must develop a strategy for operating and controlling the general secretariat. One key to this strategy is to accept the fact that the Executive Office and the White House staff are too big to be run as an informal "band of brothers." There will be hierarchy in the White House and, like it or not, a chief of staff.

The president's first obligation is to establish an organizational scheme for the staff and define a role for its chief. The chief of staff's primary purpose is to direct the White House staff and the EOP. In this capacity, the chief is more than primus inter pares among senior aides but less than grand vizier: the main task is to relieve the president of most of the purely managerial aspects of running the presidential establishment. One of the most important responsibilities is overseeing the processes of White House operations—politicking, policy making, and internal functioning—to ensure that the president gets the staff work that is needed and is not surprised by what aides are doing (or not doing) in the president's name.

The chief of staff must also be alert to protecting the president's political and institutional interests. That obligation may lead to second-guessing an ingenious staff plan to divert arms profits to the Contras or question the president's determination to make a lonely stand against Congress when compromise is necessary and possible. For the former task, the chief must be the president's eyes and ears; for the latter, sometimes a devil's advocate.

Finally, the chief of staff is responsible for preparing the president to meet congressional leaders, to face a news conference, to make an important speech, to attend a summit. The chief may not personally perform the requisite briefings but must see that they are done.

But the White House contains more people than the president and staff chief. The incumbent relies as well on senior aides and officials whose effective performance is vital to success. Therefore, the incoming president must decide on a role for the vice-president and a scheme for effective presidential management. Such a scheme would balance between the unworkable dream of "cabinet government" on one hand and the politically risky tactic of attempting to run the government from the White House on the other. Cabinet government means disjointed policy making and strong centrifugal forces in the executive branch. The Iran-Contra affair provides the latest demonstration that the White House staff is not capable of effective unilateral action. The president must learn to use the EOP to oversee and manage the executive branch, not replace it.

Therefore, new presidents must get their house in order first. The official household will play a key role in the ultimate success or failure of the administration. Therefore, the new officeholder cannot blithely appoint close loyal aides to the crucial senior staff positions and think the work has been done. Rather, the president must staff the upper levels of the general secretariat with the same care given to cabinet posts. The White House must be run with care.

One practical way to meet these responsibilities would be to adopt a simple rule of thumb in choosing and directing senior presidential aides. It may be called the "rule of defensibility": the president must choose each senior aide (say, anyone with the rank of assistant to the president) as if that officer's appointment depended on Senate confirmation; furthermore, the president and aides must ensure that whatever they do can bear congressional scrutiny.

Such a rule would provide several benefits. First, it would make it more likely that the president will get the help that is needed. Candidates for senior staff positions will be qualified for their jobs and command respect in Congress. They will possess both the political experience and the political skill to serve the chief executive effectively.

Second, staff appointees who can meet the test of this rule are likely to have friends on Capitol Hill and in the press corps. Because of these connections, they may not be solely creatures of the current president, but they will be able to help the president succeed with the powers that be in Washington. In other words, they will enhance the president's professional reputation.

Finally, the rule of defensibility will enforce reality testing at the White House. Although a president's assistants are his own, both Richard Nixon and Ronald Reagan discovered that these aides can be called before Congress if the legislature so desires. Invoking executive privilege is no defense because it smacks of hidden guilt. If senior aides or their actions cannot stand up to congressional scrutiny, then the president does not need their help.

But an orderly house is not enough. The new officeholder must go further to cope with the postmodern presidency.

Use the Transition Period to Put Your Stamp on the Government

After putting their own house in order, new presidents must turn their attention to staffing the executive branch and preparing for the stream of regulatory and judicial appointments they will make. No matter what their goals are or their criteria for selecting potential nominees, new presidents should consider the risks of not thinking strategically about personnel.

In his memoir of the Reagan presidency, Martin Anderson (1988:191–205) tells a cautionary tale of Richard Nixon's experience with executive branch appointments. According to Anderson, Nixon made a serious mistake, and realized that he was doing so, in not controlling executive appointments at the beginning of his administration. Rather, he allowed his cabinet appointees to staff their departments with a considerable degree of independence from the president-elect. Anderson contrasts that experience with Reagan's approach to appointments, which was to fill posts in such a way as to serve the president. As Richard Nathan has put it, "The essence of the Reagan approach to management is the appointment of loyal and determined policy officials" (1983:74).

Of course, Reagan's approach was controversial and not without its problems, but a new president can learn a lesson from it. Because of the importance of executive appointments to the operations of an administration and the extent of policy making by judicial and regulatory bodies, a new president must understand that personnel will translate into policy: appointments represent one of the best opportunities chief executives possess for putting their own stamp on the government.

How can the president do this? There are essentially three elements to this personnel strategy: commitment of substantial resources to the personnel operation; orientation of new appointees; and a proactive approach to finding potential appointees for judicial and regulatory posts. First, before the election, the presidential candidate ought to devote some resources to transition planning, with an eye on identifying potential nominees. Once the election is over, the president-elect should devote substantial resources to the personnel operation, which should be directed by someone competent at recruiting talent and capable of maintaining the new president's trust. This operation will continue well into the first year of the administration, if not beyond.

Second, the president-elect should ensure that new appointees receive sufficient orientation in the administration's goals and policies. Few presidents will have wide-ranging and explicit policy goals in the same manner as Ronald Reagan, but a new officeholder must be able to articulate priorities to the cabinet to ensure success. In a short time, the president-elect will be called upon to transmit those priorities to Congress, so briefing the new cabinet and other senior executive officials is a good place to begin.

Finally, the president-elect needs a proactive approach to judicial and regulatory appointments. Because of the force of vicarious policy making, the new president must give attention to the officials who will be best to fill these policy-making jobs. Therefore, the new president should construct task forces to identify potential nominees to these posts. Judicial appointments follow no schedule, but that is the precise reason why the president should attack them in advance: the sooner the job is begun, the more time there will be to find suitable candidates. Regulatory appointments are easier because they generally follow a schedule. But either will influence the direction of policy as much as or more than a cabinet officer (albeit in different ways) so a president who wants to be effective cannot merely wait for vacancies to occur.

Now the White House and the executive branch are taking shape. The new president must turn attention to policy.

Seize the Initiative in Budgeting and Policy Making

Several commentators have focused on a new president's need to seize the policy initiative by adopting what Paul Light (1982:202–3) calls a "move it or lose it" approach: the president must focus on a few top priorities at the beginning of the administration, then work hard to get them through Congress and the rest of the government. This strategy is appropriate to the postmodern presidency, with its role as chief whip in a fragmented Congress, but the key to seizing the policy initiative is to seize the budgetary initiative.

In our time, the budget has become the central instrument for governing the United States. The annual cycle of budget making is now the most fundamentally important act of the government. It not only allocates national fiscal resources but sets national priorities, influences the shape and direction of the economy, and conditions all other policy decisions made in the executive and legislative branches. Budgeting has become the focus and battleground for most of the significant and not so significant policy questions of the day, from the future of defense and arms control to education and foreign aid to labeling on frozen pizza.

Therefore, if they are to seize the policy initiative, new presidents must view the budget as their first and greatest opportunity to act. They must follow the example of Ronald Reagan and reject their predecessor's lame-duck budget proposal. This is what George Bush did in 1989, even though the lame duck in question was his former boss. Difficult as this can be to do, new presidents must create their own first budget proposal for delivery only a short time after taking office.

The lame-duck budget of the outgoing administration is poison to a new one, even if both are of the same party. A new president who does not try to change it misses the greatest opportunity available to put a stamp on the budget: the first year is when the president has the best chance of moving Congress so the first budget represents a one time opportunity. The outgoing administration had different priorities: if it is from a different party, the lame-duck proposal may be constructed to make the new administration look bad; even if it is from fellow partisans, the new president needs to put a personal imprint on things.

Ronald Reagan did not accept Jimmy Carter's last budget and insisted on developing his own proposal. As David Stockman has explained, the sheer haste in which that proposal was made contributed to future problems for the Reagan administration, but those problems were nothing compared to the missed opportunity of not submitting a budget proposal. Reagan would never have been able to achieve anything near what he wanted, nor could he have taken full advantage of his election and the honeymoon period.

But Reagan's experience points up an obstacle for the new president who wants to create a budget proposal: a serious lack of time. The new officeholder has only about six weeks in which to revise a budget document that took over a year to produce. So the new president must acquire tools to short-circuit the executive budget process. First, immediately upon election, the president-elect must request (i.e., demand) access to all budget documents of the outgoing administration. That access will facilitate the process of revision. Next, time must be bought to construct a better replacement.

Therefore, a new president should immediately request from Congress a delay of the budget process by a month or six weeks. This action will give valuable time to refine the new administration's proposals. Since this is the honeymoon period, Congress can hardly deny the new president an opportunity to do an effective job.

But if Congress balks, the new president should be prepared to bargain: additional time could be bought by promising to hold a budget summit with Congress during the period of delay. Such a summit may be a good idea even if the president is not forced into it because it will emphasize the president's attention to budgetary issues, help to reduce some of the problems that haste creates by opening budget making to congressional leaders, ease passage of this first budget, and counteract the centrifugal forces in Congress that complicate the president's job. A summit limits the number of congressional players involved in budgeting and enhances the influence of congressional leaders—a plus for the chief whip trying to deal with the new Congress.

However it is acquired, the new president needs time to put together a budget proposal so as to be able to seize the initiative in shaping the single most important tool of public policy. It will not guarantee success, but it will be the key to the rest of policy making.

Make the Most of the Postmodern Presidency

Having come to understand the revised nature of the office, the incoming president should make the most of what it provides. That does not mean an attempt to expand the prerogatives of the office to the exclusion of congressional power or that "going public" carries no risks, but the new incumbent will have to accept that the office wears a particular shape and is not easily malleable. The new president must learn to live with the prerogatives of the postmodern presidency.

The prerogatives of the contemporary office, from PUPD to administrative clearance and top-down budgeting, are not uncontroversial, but it is no accident that several recent presidents sought to develop them. The predecessors of the new president were trying to free themselves from the limits on their influence imposed by the growth of the bureaucracy, the congressional revolution of the mid-1970s, the growing importance of budgetary issues, and the difficulties of making foreign policy in the post-Vietnam era. Their solution, these postmodern prerogatives, have their risks, but they represent rational responses to the president's environment.

Therefore, before discarding these new powers, the new president should give thought to how they can be turned to advantage. For example, administrative clearance can be turned to liberal purposes as well as conservative ones. In the Reagan administration, administrative clearance was used to target new regulations proposed by the Environmental Protection Agency, but the Department of Defense was exempt from the process. A Democratic president might extend the clearance process to Defense and use it as part of a larger effort at military reform.

Likewise, top-down budgeting is a tool that would suit any president's priorities. It allows the chief executive to put a personal stamp on the executive budget process, whatever that stamp may be. In this age of the budget as the central instrument for governing, the president has little choice but to run executive budget making from the White House.

The new president should thus consider how the contemporary presidential office can be used to advance goals, thereby making the most of the position.

The Postmodern Presidency in the American System

In the late twentieth century, American chief executives are postmodern presidents. They attempt to govern through a mix of prerogative power, public politics, and old-fashioned bargaining. They focus much of their attention on budgeting and regulation because they live in a governing system that operates through these devices. But their appointments, whether consciously or not, also contribute to each incumbent's ultimate impact on the nation.

Postmodern presidents need to be better managers than their predecessors were. Whereas the modern presidency was thought to be a position of legislative leadership requiring a master lawmaker, the contemporary office is more a position of administration and management. For that reason, as well as changes in the presidential nominating system, governors and other executives once again make good candidates for the nation's highest office.

Whoever steps into the Oval Office in these late-century years must be skilled at running a large bureaucracy—not the executive branch but the Executive Office of the President—and so must possess extensive management skills. The first order of business for these incumbents, regardless of party or policy goals, is to set their own house in order.

Unless presidents take this first step, they will be overwhelmed by a governing system and a political environment that has many centers of power: in a fragmented Congress, in the courts and regulatory commissions, in the executive bureaucracy, in a profusion of interest groups, in the media, in the states, and, finally, in the White House. Beyond American borders is a changing international environment in which the role of the United States is not yet clear, so the president's place in world affairs is also in flux. The president's environment of diffused power can be influenced, but only if the incumbent knows the rules and how to play the game. By adopting the political strategy outlined here, the postmodern president may be able to excel at the game.

5 PRESIDENTIAL PERSUASIVENESS AND PUBLIC SECTOR LEADERSHIP

Marcia Lynn Whicker and Todd W. Areson

Modern Presidents and the Honeymoon Period

Presidents as the nation's chief executive set the tone for their administrations during the early days, a tone that influences the administration's effectiveness throughout its first term. Equally, and perhaps for this reason, the public looks to the president as the chief spokesperson for the federal establishment. These realities emphasize the importance of newly elected presidents "getting off on the right foot," using the powers of the presidency to be as persuasive as possible.

Traditionally, presidents are given a "honeymoon" period by both the press and the public in the early days of their administrations, during which time praise flows more liberally than criticism. Skillful presidents have used the honeymoon to establish priorities, convey them to the nation, and persuade Congress, the press, and the American people at large to become team players in implementing the president's vision for the country (Edwards and Wayne, 1985:109–10).

President John F. Kennedy used his honeymoon period to recruit "the best and the brightest" to government service and to excite the nation with a vision of a New Frontier—in space, in civil rights, and in foreign relations (Burns, 1984:74–79; Halberstam, 1972). Lyndon Johnson, propelled to the presidency by the assassination of Kennedy, enjoyed an unusually long honeymoon because of the tragic circumstances surrounding his ascension to the White House. In 1964, Johnson used this continuing popular support, coupled with his massive electoral mandate, to push through major civil rights and antipoverty legislation (Kearns, 1972; Reedy, 1982; Divine, 1981). More recently, Ronald Reagan used his honeymoon to cut federal income taxes drastically and to implement other aspects of supply-side economics.

In a short period, Reagan shifted the nation's agenda from a liberal one, oriented toward social and redistributive programs, to a conservative one, intent on reestablishing a strong U.S. military role abroad (Jones, 1988).

As he entered his honeymoon period, President George Bush confronted a number of problems that undercut his ability to establish and implement his policy goals rapidly. Electoral pundits did not interpret Bush's margin as a mandate because he won only 54 percent of the popular vote, because of citizens' disenchantment with the presidential candidates and their negative campaigns, and because, for the first time, the losing party in the presidential election gained seats in both the House and the Senate. Campaign coverage during 1988, though addressing major issues confronting the nation, had a clearly negative cast reflective of the campaigns. What came through in the media was an inordinate focus on the trivial personal "horse race." Unlike his predecessor, Ronald Reagan, Bush lacked the polished performance skills that Reagan had used to extend his honeymoon period.

Bush faced an opposition Congress. Further, Democrats were belligerent, nonconciliatory, and put off by the effective hardball tactics and negative advertising used by the Bush campaign. Finally, his earlier selection of Dan Quayle as a running mate, without benefit of advice from his closest advisers, cast doubt on both Bush's judgment and his decision-making style (*Washington Post*, 1988).

Even more ominous for President Bush were the massive twin federal and trade deficits—a legacy of the Reagan revolution. These deficits would effectively handcuff any president, especially one following eight years of the "great communicator." Thus Bush lacked a clear mandate to use with Congress to implement the cautious change advocated by the public, change that would simultaneously maintain the prosperity of the Reagan years and address the nagging fiscal problems of government.

What behaviors have enhanced the ability of the nation's chief executive to persuade Congress, the public, and the press to pursue his policy goals? An examination of honeymoon periods of modern presidents, emphasizing those since 1960 as well as including the presidencies of Herbert Hoover and Franklin D. Roosevelt, reveals several conditions that increase presidential persuasiveness and capacity to govern. Some attributes deal with the message; others involve characteristics of the messenger.

Attributes of Presidential Persuasion: Dealing with the Message

The message must be simple. Especially in recent years, the public has become accustomed to receiving information on issues in "sound bites" on the evening news (Edwards and Wayne, 1985:156; Edelman, 1974; Rockman, 1984:200; Polsby and Wildavsky, 1984:187–88). Even the sound bites are shrinking in size. Two recent studies document that one-liners have decreased from an average of forty-five seconds ten years ago to fifteen seconds in 1984 and still further to nine seconds in 1988—an 80 percent decrease (Alter, 1988). The "KISS" theory—Keep It Simple, Stupid—long a dictum of basic communication, applies to presidential persuasiveness as much as to that of any other chief executive (Rockman, 1984:200; Edwards and Wayne, 1985:93). This element of persuasiveness does not preclude complex solutions to complicated problems but does imply that the communication of those efforts must be simple and straightforward.

Bush's comments about being the "education president" and wanting a "kinder, gentler" America were tailored to sound-bite size—effectively conveying an image in few words. In the campaign, Bush used the sound-bite technique to his advantage and to the detriment of his opponent, Governor Michael Dukakis, by hanging several images on Dukakis—the Pledge of Allegiance distortion, the Massachusetts "revolving door" furlough program symbolized by Willie Horton, Boston Harbor's pollution symbolizing Dukakis's position on the environment, and the rabid-liberal image of Dukakis as a "card-carrying member" of the American Civil Liberties Union.

The message must convey clear and limited priorities. Presidents who overload the national agenda during their first few weeks in office fail to communicate a clear and manageable agenda behind which the public can unite. President Jimmy Carter failed to limit his agenda to manageable proportions and consequently lost an opportunity to convey clear priorities. By contrast, Reagan arrived in the Oval Office with a clear agenda to cut taxes, to reduce regulation and the role of government, and to increase defense spending. Bush did not use his campaign to create a mandate to address a limited number of key issues. Nor as president did he initially present a limited agenda to the press and public, talking instead about a variety of issues ranging from new programs in education, child care, and environmental cleanup to waging war on drugs and creating new weapons systems.

The message must be hopeful and optimistic. Optimism as a motivator is easier to sustain for the long run than pessimism. Out-group and scapegoat techniques work better to demobilize opposition forces in the short run than to motivate one's own troops in the long run. President Carter's now famous "malaise in America" speech, intended to motivate people to overcome problems, had the opposite effect. It was given in opposition to the counsel of many of his closest advisers (Strong, 1986). Reagan, in contrast, constantly gave upbeat, optimistic speeches that discussed the successes of individuals in the face of massive societal problems (Barber, 1985:494–96). His emphasis on "pride in America" restored the public's faith in itself and in the country. Having engaged in a negative, "low-road" campaign, Bush had no choice but to shift to positive images and speeches, to take advantage of and extend his honeymoon period.

Unifying messages are more persuasive than divisive messages. Effective presidents, like all persuasive chief executives, are team and coalition builders who unite their supporters, even across major cleavages (Smith, 1982). Reagan began the process of pulling "Reagan Democrats"—blue-collar and ethnic voters—into the Republican party by appealing to patriotic and unifying themes (Ornstein, Kohut, and McCarthy, 1988:16–19). Democrats, who have stressed care of the poor, homeless, and minorities, have emphasized differences among major subgroups and been less persuasive in recent elections (Polsby and Wildavsky, 1984).

Unifying presidents are more likely to be temperamentally conservative and incremental. They are most likely to appear in times when there is no great outcry for change. Past experience and a track record of success contribute to a president's image as a unifier (Rockman, 1984:198).

Bush has had to confront the delicate problem of needing to unify the Republican base further, to cope with broadening gaps between the rich and the underclass, the well educated and the illiterate, and light-skinned and dark-skinned Americans. Yet he has had to do so while appealing to common concerns rather than to zero-sum politics and divisiveness.

Persuasive messages link appeals to sacrifice with promises of gain. Especially in recent decades, Americans have become accustomed to rising living standards and advertising appeals to their self-interest (Leakachman, 1982). In an era of instant credit and short-term gratification, sacrifice is not commonly expected or called for. Not since Kennedy, in building his New Frontier, admonished Americans to ask not what their country could do for them but what they could do for their country has a U.S. president so blatantly appealed to the motive of personal sacrifice for national gain.

The U.S. capitalistic system is predicated on notions of individual profit and gain (Ferguson, 1971). Juxtaposing a self-interested, profit-driven capitalist economy with political rhetoric calling for pain and loss seems both incongruous and distasteful in the minds of citizens, even if necessary. Bush, in dealing with the twin deficits, avoided calling for tax increases through early 1990, thus eschewing any mention of political pain. Yet experts questioned whether this approach, since abandoned, would lead to long-term economic decay if not to more immediate disaster. When Bush did retract his read-my-lips promise of no new taxes, he attempted to link proposed tax increases clearly with the benefits to be gained from such actions.

Messages that contrast sharply with the policies of the previous chief executive are more persuasive than those that advocate continuity. Presidents regarded as most persuasive, in retrospect, have presented messages that sharply contrasted with the messages of their predecessors. Kennedy's bold New Frontier advocated bearing any burden to bring freedom to the rest of the world and revamping society at home to address social inequities. His message contrasted markedly with Dwight D. Eisenhower's mandate to pull back from international intervention, especially in Korea, and return the country to normalcy after two wars in two decades (Barber, 1985:254–98, 140–47). Reagan's optimistic and patriotic "Morning in America" message sharply differed from Carter's theme of "malaise." Carter told the American people that their government could not do everything; Reagan believed that it should do less domestically (e.g., proposing to abolish the education and energy departments) and with fewer employees.

Part of the appeal of sharp contrast is that a media-reared public gets accustomed to constant bombardment by new images, messages, advertisements, films, and themes (Grossman and Kumar, 1981:231). Contrast is interesting; continuity is boring (Edwards and Wayne, 1985:155–59). Also relevant is that social conditions change, and new messages are often more appropriate than old ones. Initially, Bush was viewed as largely an extension of the Reagan revolution and its policies. He was selected as the appropriate caretaker of Reagan's conservative agenda.

Messages that appeal to basic as well as to higher-level needs are more persuasive than those appealing to higher needs only. Abraham Maslow (1970) developed a hierarchy of needs in which he posits five major levels: physical, safety, social, esteem, and self-actualization. Until adequately satisfied, lower-level needs are more powerful than higher-level needs as motivators of human behavior. For individuals to be predominantly concerned with the higher-level issues of esteem or self-actualization, they must provide an adequate level of satisfaction for their lower-level needs.

Presidential messages that combine appeals to lower-level needs with those to higher-level needs, then, are more persuasive than those appealing only to higher-level needs. For example, appeals to national security and defense are generally persuasive, especially when peace has prevailed in the preceding years (Hinckley, 1985:187–88). In most instances, citizens view national defense as promoting national safety and aligned with their own needs for personal safety. Ironically, antiwar movements also appeal to the lower-level need of personal safety, but individuals have placed personal safety above national safety when forced to choose. By emphasizing national defense and promising to buy all new weapons systems in the planning and development pipeline, Bush emphasized these safety needs more than his opponent did. His forceful actions and rapid escalation of U.S. involvement in the Persian Gulf to military intervention intensified concern for national defense and safety issues. Consequently, Bush's popularity at home soared to a record high.

Attributes of Presidential Persuasion: Dealing with the Messenger

Presidents perceived as strong and competent are more persuasive than those perceived as weak and ineffective. Leadership skills are intimately tied to presidential persuasiveness (Herzik and Dodson, 1982). Presidents regarded as strong, decisive, and confident are perceived as better leaders, more capable of achieving their stated objectives and policies, than those perceived as weak, indecisive, and hesitant. Richard Nixon, often unlikable and by some standards devious, was still perceived as strong until the Watergate scandal undermined his public support. He used this strength to convince the public to reverse its official orientation toward Red China and to withdraw from Vietnam on a delayed schedule (Whicker and Moore 1988:111–12).

Carter, by contrast, was perceived as weak, plebian, obsessed with details, and ineffectual. He was not able to persuade Congress to pass his initiatives or to gain wide public support for many of his policies (Burns, 1984:57). Reagan enjoyed widespread public support, partially based on his stage presence and avuncular nature. He used this strength to push his agenda through the Congress (Fishel, 1985:204).

In the early stages of his presidential campaign, Bush worked under the handicap of being perceived as weak, ineffectual, and wimpish, despite a record as a successful businessman, war hero, and high-level public manager. By the end of the campaign, he had turned this image around so that the public perceived him as the stronger and more competent candidate. This turnaround, however, was brought about by negative, divisive tactics, a short-run approach. To extend his honeymoon, Bush had to be able to create an image of strength based on constructive accomplishments.

Presidents who present themselves as part of an orderly decision-making apparatus are more persuasive than those who present themselves as always personally in charge. Reagan was often called the "Teflon" president because his public blunders and misstatements did not stick to him, causing him to suffer political repercussions. In part, this Teflon quality arose from Reagan's ability to project himself as the chief executive of an orderly, efficient corporate structure that would carry on, even when he faltered. Recognizing that presidents are only human, the public believes that no one person can be omniscient, always making the best decision. Nor, given the

American bias against strong authority, does it want such an "infallible" leader.

Presidents who present themselves as laboring alone against the rising tide of dissent, chaos, and destructive forces more readily challenge the public's credulity. Alistair Cooke has noted that "all Presidents start out pretending to run a crusade, but after a couple of years, they find they are running something much less heroic, much more intractable: namely the Presidency" (Cronin, 1980:143).

Although the public likes the image of strength in its presidents, this strength should be based in large part on the president's command of an effective White House and administration and should not reside solely in individual vigilance (Hess, 1988). Good presidents are good team builders and team players; persuasive presidents also have these characteristics (Burns, 1984:177). Bush has earned good marks on this score, having spent most of his public career as a team player and agency executive.

The persuasive president is a good media performer. Franklin D. Roosevelt, John F. Kennedy, and Ronald Reagan have been among our best presidents in using the media to accomplish their purposes (Whicker and Moore, 1988:69–71). Jimmy Carter and Gerald Ford were less effective media performers and less persuasive presidents (Kerbel, 1986; Smoller, 1986). Increasingly, presidents need to use the media to communicate their priorities not only to the public but also to the Congress, the press, and peer world leaders (Edwards, 1983). In many crucial ways, the media have replaced political parties as the gatekeepers for political success.

Presidential scholars have long recognized that the relationship between press and president is one of mutual manipulation (Rubin, 1981). Our more persuasive presidents have been more successful than the press in this manipulation (Barber, 1980:8–12). Bush has not been regarded as a good media performer, lacking the pizzazz and polish of a Reagan. During his campaign, however, he compensated by hiring good media and advertising consultants. This approach for effective communication works less well in running the White House, however, than in running a campaign (Smith, 1988).

The persuasive president demonstrates an understanding of the issues. Persuasiveness depends on presenting a coherent message. To be persuasive, presidents must have a clear understanding of the issues so they can communicate their essence to crucial audiences. They combine expert knowledge, culture-based sentiment, and short-term political realities into ideas about issues that contain both emotive and intellectual content (Hargrove and Nelson, 1984:75–78). Inundated with information, signals, and demands from many quarters, persuasive presidents are quick studies, able to ask the key questions, extract the major dimensions of a problem or proposal, frame reasonable solutions, and express these important points succinctly. Presidents need a fundamental knowledge base of public sector problems, traditions, and institutions as well as great intellectual capacity to be able to do this. Roosevelt, Truman, Kennedy, Johnson, and Nixon all demonstrated this ability. Though Bush was not an intellectual, his background and previous career experiences rightly indicated that he too could sort out the trivial from the important and convey the latter. This capacity was especially demonstrated during the Gulf war.

The persuasive president creates a vision of the future, which becomes the operating framework guiding the administration. As chief executives, presidents need to excite the populace with a vision and sense of direction for the country (Barber, 1980:322). Persuasive presidents must not only create a national agenda but also provide the means for implementing their vision through programs and policies. The New Deal, Fair Deal, New Frontier, and Great Society were visions painted by modern presidents. Reagan painted a view of a "Norman Rockwell" America. Until he began to wage war in the Persian Gulf, Bush did not clearly address what he meant by "the vision thing."

Persuasive presidents motivate their followers by demonstrating enthusiasm and manipulating emotion-laden symbols. Visions are often communicated by symbols and myths. Reagan was a master at using patriotic symbols to convey his vision of a stronger, revitalized nation. This mastery and his own unabashed pride in the United States engendered a contagious public enthusiasm that helped him implement his agenda. Carter, by contrast, confronted with a public weary of presidential imperialism and regality, adopted symbols of the common man, wearing sweaters when talking to the nation on television, walking to his inauguration, and curtailing the use of limousines for top officials (Hess, 1988:141). Only belatedly did Carter realize that he had demythologized the presidency more than the public wanted or would allow. Johnson used symbols from his Texas roots to convey a larger-than-life sense of the White House and its power. Kennedy used the arts and symbols of youth to convey a sense of vigor, vitality, and hope.

During his campaign, Bush used the negative symbols of environmental pollution and crime and even converted a normally positive symbol—the Pledge of Allegiance—into a question of patriotism. He won electoral victory, however, with the positive symbols of peace and prosperity.

Persuasive presidents use a sense of humor. One of the ways in which presidents communicate effectively is through humor (Edwards and Wayne, 1985:99). Humor can be used not only to entertain but also to garner empathy from the press and public and to deflect hostility and criticism for stances that might be unpopular. Among modern presidents, Kennedy stands out as the most effective in using humor to deflect hostile and unwanted queries, especially at press conferences.

Reagan also proved adept at both off-the-cuff and canned humor. Both of these presidents used self-deprecating humor well to evoke empathy from the press and the public. During his eight years as vice-president and during the 1988 presidential campaign, Bush did not demonstrate skill at using humor to persuade.

Persuasive presidents have a sense of history. Persuasive presidents have a sense of timing and an ability to distinguish the important from the less important that derive from a broad sense of history (Cronin, 1980:144). This enables them to place their administrations in the context of American and world history and to set appropriate future directions for the nation. This sense also provides a connectedness for the populace, reducing feelings of isolation and aloneness that can result when crises and situations are viewed as insulated from time and surroundings.

Since historical events flow in cycles, presidents with a sense of history have a finely tuned sense of timing and of what is needed and will appeal to the populace at any particular point. Presidents with this skill are "transforming leaders"—they elevate citizens beyond the immediacy of daily issues and concerns (Burns, 1984). Before his presidency, Bush did not demonstrate a strong sense of history; he could be defined more properly as a process-oriented problem solver. The outbreak of war against Iraq early in 1991, however, demonstrated that his education at Yale University, his broad base of experience, and his previous years of government service had furnished him with a greater sense of how historical cycles work than some more recent occupants of the White House.

A Model of Presidential Persuasiveness:
Message and Messenger

As described above, attributes of presidential persuasiveness fall into two categories: characteristics of the message and those of the messenger. Considering these major categories and the modern presidents, we can create a model of presidential persuasiveness that divides the continuous dimensions for both message and messenger into two discrete categories—high and low. Crossing these two dimensions creates a four-celled typology (see Figure 5.1).

The most desirable cell in which presidents may be located is high on both dimensions. In this cell, presidents with persuasive personal attributes deliver persuasive messages. The least desirable category is low on both dimensions so that neither the personal attributes of presidents nor their messages are persuasive. Sometimes a dichotomy exists; presidents may be

Figure 5.1. Model of Presidential Persuasiveness

		Persuasiveness of Message	
		Low	High
Persuasiveness of Messenger	High	Eisenhower Johnson	Roosevelt Kennedy Reagan
	Low	Hoover Ford Carter	Truman Nixon

high on personal attributes and low on message persuasiveness, or vice versa. This model may be used to help scholars and political pundits judge the potential success of future presidents and presidential candidates before they assume office. The categories in the model may be more fully illustrated with the persuasive attributes of recent presidents.

High Message and High Messenger Persuasiveness

Three modern presidents—Roosevelt, Kennedy, and Reagan—were persuasive as messengers and presented convincing and appealing messages.

ROOSEVELT. In a time of conflict and turmoil, Roosevelt came to power on the promise that he would engage in ambitious strategies to relieve the misery confronting a nation in the throes of the Depression. Telling the people that the only thing they had to fear was fear itself, he proposed unifying reforms that gave hope to the downtrodden and relief to the unemployed. His proposals for Social Security, unemployment insurance, old age pensions, assisting labor organization, aiding farmers, regulating stock and financial markets, and providing electricity to the Tennessee Valley through the Tennessee Valley Authority were optimistic and hopeful. Yet despite the profusion of programs, the message remained simple and the priorities clear—to combat the Depression, revitalize the economy, and diminish human misery.

In addition to advocating a persuasive message that the country wanted to hear, Roosevelt was a persuasive messenger. He used humor, hope, and his personal vigor to revitalize a depressed, stalled nation. He conveyed a sense of acting on problems within a spirit of experimentation—failures resulting from action were better than no action at all. As a media performer, he ushered in a new era of presidential communication via the radio, using his Fireside Chats to comfort, inform, and reenergize the public. He also instituted press conferences in the Oval Office, making himself the chief White House spokesperson to the press. Through his performances, he renewed the public's faith in itself and in the capacity of government to solve pressing problems. In his corporate role, he brought to government an impressive array of talented individuals to direct his New Deal programs and gave them leeway to think creatively. He intuitively understood that balanced-budget principles could be violated, becoming the first Keynesian president.

KENNEDY. Like Roosevelt, Kennedy conveyed a hopeful, optimistic message of America's invincibility throughout the world. Linking the burdens of defense to promises of anticommunist strength, Kennedy told the nation that no burden was too great to bear for the banner of peace and freedom. Richard Neustadt, a Kennedy adviser, admonished the youthful and handsome president to follow the spirit of Roosevelt's presidential style and message (Hess, 1988:74–87). Kennedy presented clearly his priorities of protecting freedom, combating communism, exploring space, and advancing civil rights as part of his New Frontier. His interventionist and activist message marked a sharp contrast to that of Eisenhower, his predecessor, who pulled the United States out of the Korean War, warned against the expansion of the military-industrial complex, and was quiescent on social reforms.

Kennedy as a messenger was highly persuasive. He presented an image of competence, strength, youthful vigor, and intelligence. His Pulitzer Prize–winning book, *Profiles in Courage*, demonstrated a sense of history and an appreciation for the past. He was the first to participate in unscripted, televised press conferences, showing a mastery of the issues of the day. During various public performances, especially his press conferences, he used humor to win the affection and loyalty of the press and public. His New Frontier provided a bold vision of a future in which poverty was reduced and freedom increased.

REAGAN. More than any recent president, Reagan came to the White House with a clear and limited agenda—to increase defense spending, cut taxes, and reduce the size of government. His message of "Morning in America" was optimistic and renewing and provided a sharp contrast to Carter's "malaise" and emphasis on resource limitations. He unified the nation and restored its faith. By emphasizing appropriate spending on defense, he appealed to basic safety needs. In foreign policy, his Grenada and Qaddafi policies of "shoot first and ask questions later" recaptured an earlier "macho" sense of national pride.

As messenger, Reagan appeared comfortable and strong. Using a triumvi-

rate to substitute for a strong, single chief of staff during his first administration and developing an advisory and decision-making system of cabinet
council government, he presented himself as the nation's chief executive
officer, willing to delegate responsibility to trusted aides. He constantly
used individual stories, often of the genre of the Horatio Alger success myth
and of private charity to help the needy, as symbols of his conservative ideology and bootstrapping perspective. Cracking jokes, even immediately
after he was shot in an assassination attempt, Reagan used humor effectively. His Hollywood career made him an effective media performer in
arenas where he could rely on a script. Ironically, though not known for his
understanding of the issues, he did have excellent staging skills. His fifty
news conferences were highly structured, lasting precisely thirty minutes
each (Pfiffner, 1990). By holding a limited number of press conferences, his
staff protected him from settings in which he performed less well.

Low Message and High Messenger Persuasiveness

EISENHOWER. Left with the legacy of the Roosevelt and Truman reforms, Eisenhower was unable to abolish them and not eager to extend
them. His social and economic policies contrasted little with those of his
predecessors. Change occurred by inertia and drift. Eisenhower was not interested in extending civil rights. He appointed Earl Warren—the liberal
U.S. Supreme Court justice who extended civil liberties for criminal defen-
dants and oversaw the 1954 *Brown* v. *Board of Education* decision that over-
turned the "separate but equal" doctrine of racial segregation in public
schools—under the erroneous impression that Warren would pursue a conservative philosophy. Eisenhower, the superb general, did little to chart the
nation's course during his eight years in the White House. During those
years, the nation drifted into the McCarthy period of suspicion, innuendo,
blacklisting, and fear of reprisal for anyone charged with communist connections (Richardson, 1979; Reichard, 1975; Melanson and Mayers, 1987).

By contrast, as a former general and war hero who led the Allied forces to
victory against the Axis during World War II, Eisenhower exhibited many
characteristics of an effective messenger. He was perceived as competent
and strong, even to the point of stubbornness when pushed in a direction he
did not embrace. He appointed Sherman Adams as a strong chief of staff and
preferred to delegate much responsibility to his subordinates, using the military model of hierarchical command. As civilian commander in chief, he
viewed the role of president as that of chief executive rather than politician
and party leader. He created a vision of a middle-class America in which
laissez-faire and family values dominated for much of the decade. Though

not particularly effective at using humor, he did inspire confidence by his straightforwardness and national pride.

JOHNSON. Lyndon Johnson, like Eisenhower, was effective as a messenger. The message, his profusion of programs in both domestic and foreign affairs, was, at times, overwhelming. Unable to set priorities between the Great Society and the Vietnam conflict, Johnson tried to choose both guns and butter. His message in both arenas was divisive. In social policy, his message advocated much-needed reforms in civil rights but nonetheless wrought great divisions and conflicts in the nation's social fabric. The conflict his Vietnam policies created split the nation into bitter camps, denying him the opportunity to run as an incumbent in 1968. The 1968 Democratic national convention in Chicago remains unparalleled in its street violence and dissension. Nor did Johnson ever effectively link in the public mind the sacrifices being made in Vietnam with the national gain expected to occur as a result of U.S. involvement. The public as well as many in his administration remained unclear about the U.S. purpose there.

As a well-tempered politican, Johnson understood issues, politics, and the use of the media. He created a vision of a Great Society, in which civil liberties would be available to minorities, education greatly improved, and poverty abolished. Having lived and worked for decades in the crucible of the nation's capital, he had a strong sense of history. His position as Senate majority leader gave him a vantage point from which to watch the issues affecting the nation unfold. He used humor on occasion, especially in his early years in office before Vietnam became a political cancer. He was perceived as strong. Though less skilled at performing for the public and press, he gave command performances for congressmen and senators, passing much of the legislation Kennedy initiated but did not live to see implemented.

High Message and Low Messenger Persuasiveness

TRUMAN. Harry Truman inherited Roosevelt's initiatives and programs and added the Marshall Plan for reconstructing Europe as well as a plan for rebuilding Japan. He also instituted the Truman Doctrine of containment of communism, including aid to Greece, Turkey, and the North Atlantic Treaty Organization, to fight Soviet aggression. Setting anticommunism as a top national priority, he pursued these policies, even to the point of involving the United States in military conflict in Korea and, some would argue, in starting the Cold War. His message of using U.S. economic and military assistance abroad to support free peoples and anticommunist interests was simple and grasped by the public. Although both houses of Congress were controlled by the Republicans during his first two years in office, the appeal of his programs helped him enact much of his Fair Deal.

Truman was less effective as a messenger. He barely won election in 1948. The margin was so small that some newspapers had already printed headlines declaring his opponent, New York Governor Thomas E. Dewey, the victor before the final votes were tabulated. He was catapulted into the presidency in 1945 by Roosevelt's death and lacked the long exposure to national politics and the hunger for the office that many presidents have before entering the White House. His style was regarded as abrupt and blunt. His intense partisanship and his race against a "do-nothing Congress" contributed frequently to tense relationships with that body. His salty style and contentiousness with the press brought mixed reviews of his media performances. Unlike Eisenhower, he did not adopt a corporate management style but rather used a personal approach to policy development and program implementation. His popularity with the public declined so much during his first term that many Democratic leaders sought to replace him as the Democratic candidate in 1948. His failure to run in 1952 reflected a mixed public response to Truman's presidential persuasiveness.

NIXON. Despite his personal flaws, enemies' lists, and moral lapses on Watergate, Richard Nixon, like Truman, presented the right message at the right time to the American people and to his peer world leaders. Only Truman rivals him as a manager of foreign policy (Whicker and Moore, 1988:111–12). His message was simple: remove the United States from involvement in Vietnam, preferably through negotiated peace rather than unilateral defeat. Although many grew impatient with delays and a four-year prolongment of the Asian war, this priority was clearly expressed and offered hope to a badly divided and demoralized American public. Although domestic conflict continued over the proper time and approach for withdrawal, the message that the United States was prepared to withdraw short of victory was unifying and applied balm to festering sores of political dissent.

In a bold and open break with past policy, Nixon pressed for opening relations with the People's Republic of China and maintained competent and realistic relations with the Eastern Soviet bloc. During the Nixon administration, negotiations for SALT I—the first Strategic Arms Limitation Treaty—were begun and completed, representing a major step toward the control of nuclear weapons. Nixon's foreign policy initiatives appealed to both lower-level safety and higher-level needs.

As a messenger, Nixon fared less well. He never succeeded in developing a fluid and natural performance style, instead looking strained, awkward, and shifty. Nor did he have good relations with the media; those relations were characterized by an absence of trust, humor, playfulness, and give-and-take.

He appeared moralistic, duty-bound, heavy-bearded, and at times haggard.

As the Watergate scandal progressed in his second term, Nixon's relations with the press and public fell to an all-time low, and impeachment appeared imminent. Forced to resign rather than face an impeachment trial and accused of lying, chicanery, and obstruction of justice, the Watergate-embattled Nixon was the antithesis of strength and competence. Although Nixon did demonstrate a masterful understanding of foreign affairs, he did not exhibit the same interest in domestic issues. He was able to manipulate public opinion successfully on at least one occasion, with his Checkers speech to save his political career and remain as Eisenhower's vice-president, but he was not particularly skilled at manipulating symbols during his presidency.

Low Message and Low Messenger Persuasiveness

HOOVER. Neither Hoover's message nor his presidential style was persuasive to a nation in economic difficulty. He was a pessimist, seeing half-empty rather than half-full glasses. Personally, he suffered from depression, contributing to his gloomy outlook. His balanced-budget message represented a continuation of, rather than a break with, past policies. In part because he was not open and communicative, Hoover had difficulty establishing clear priorities. By stressing fiscal responsibility over hunger and the need for jobs, Hoover ignored the basic human needs of much of the population, and the unemployment rate rose to 25 percent by the end of his administration. Nor did he link the sacrifices he asked of those hardest hit by the Depression with the benefits he expected them to gain from a balanced-budget, laissez-faire approach to government responsibility. Mastering immense amounts of information and doing his "homework" thoroughly, he tended to flood his policy-making audiences with facts rather than to present a simple message and involve them in the decision-making process.

He made little use of symbols or humor. He was a poor media performer, eschewing politics and treating government as a bloodless business. He was not comfortable performing publicly, especially on radio. According to James D. Barber, "Hoover never could swallow the logic that recognizes that leadership demands rhetoric, that rhetoric demands drama, and that drama demands artifice" (1980:58). The ultimate detail man, he lacked a sense of humor. He failed to create a better vision of the future for a nation that desperately needed such a vision. As his administration deteriorated, he continued ineffective appeals to restore public confidence and did not manipulate symbols or present new options to generate this confidence.

FORD. Gerald Ford was an accidental president. He was appointed to the vice-presidency by Nixon in 1973, to replace the disgraced Spiro Agnew, under the provisions of the Twenty-Fifth Amendment. In August 1974, when Nixon resigned under threat of impeachment, Ford was involuntarily escalated to the presidency. He had no message beyond restoring decency and confidence in government and the presidency, a goal he fulfilled. His response to "stagflation" resulting from simultaneously rising inflation and unemployment, the voluntary Whip Inflation Now (WIN) program, failed to link sacrifice to gain or to win widespread popular support.

Nor was Ford's image as presidential messenger one of strength and competence. Despite Ford's previous skill as an athlete, the media focused on his stumbles. He failed effectively to counter Carter's charges in the preelection 1976 presidential debates. Nor did he demonstrate mastery of the issues, identifying Poland as a noncommunist country in those debates. In his long-term experience as House minority leader, he did not polish his public performance skills to a level Americans expect of presidents. And during his short two years in the White House, he was unable to demonstrate more than an awkward sense of humor or a limited sense of history.

CARTER. Carter also ranks low for both his message and his style. Inundating the public with detailed programs and scattered policies immediately upon assuming office, he failed to create a sense of clear national priorities. He shifted his foreign affairs focus, moving from a policy emphasizing problems of North-South, developed–less developed nations to a more traditional and conservative one, emphasizing East-West relations. After a thaw, he adopted a Cold War stance toward the Soviet Union when it invaded Afghanistan, pulling the United States out of the 1980 Olympics, held in Moscow, and embargoing the sale of U.S. grain to the USSR. At times, his message was pessimistic, especially when dealing with the energy crisis and domestic trends. His human rights emphasis in foreign affairs, though laudable, was not linked to appeals to basic national safety needs.

Carter's style was perceived as sometimes less than presidential. Though he overcame a speech impediment, Carter remained a pedestrian media performer. His television presentations, an attempt to draw on Roosevelt's tradition of Fireside Chats, were wooden and singsongy. He micromanaged, focusing too much on details rather than on broader, consistent policies. Because of his unwillingness to delegate, he did not use a corporate structure to handle lesser problems. The Iranian hostage crisis created a public image of Carter as ineffective and impotent. Known for his public display of religious and moral convictions, he did not use humor effectively. Although Carter did seem to understand the specifics of various issues, especially foreign affairs, he did not use his knowledge to present a vision of a better and stronger America. His attempt to symbolize the need for austerity and conservation in energy use by wearing sweaters and turning White House thermostats down proved ineffective.

Conclusion

The major shifts of policy that the United States confronts, especially moving from a national to an international economy and agenda, will call for strong and persuasive presidential leadership. The most persuasive future presidents will be those high on both dimensions—message and messenger. Presidents not high on both dimensions may adopt behaviors and policies that increase their effectiveness; yet the likelihood that they will do so remains small. Once politicians achieve sufficient national stature to mount a credible campaign for the White House, their personal style has usually been set. Although personal change is possible, it is less probable than changes that affect the persuasiveness of the message. Changes in the presentation and content of the message are more likely, but they may be perceived as incongruent with earlier messages. The fact that only three of the past ten presidents were high on both dimensions makes it a less than even bet that future presidents will be able to meet the nation's needs.

6 FEDERALISM AND ADMINISTRATIVE DISCRETION

William H. Stewart

Federalism in the United States usually has been considered in the context of conflict and cooperation between the federal government and state governments viewed as whole entities. Originally, the content of the constitutional doctrines of federalism was defined through judicial decisions, principally decisions of the U.S. Supreme Court. Even today, there is inadequate recognition of the relationship between competing models of operational federalism and the power position of public administrators, especially administrators in state and local bureaucracies. It is the general thesis of this chapter that the conception of the American federal system which is dominant in any particular period, especially as enunciated by the president and Congress, has important implications for the roles of administrators, particularly in determining the kinds and amounts of discretion they are able to exercise and the leadership opportunities they will be able to take advantage of. Coleman Ransone was, of course, primarily concerned with state governors and the multiple dimensions of leadership associated with the gubernatorial office. This essay is focused on elected political but also on bureaucratic leadership.

Several important issues pertaining to executive leadership are discussed in this chapter in the context of four historically and contemporaneously noteworthy concepts of intergovernmental relations. Administrative decision-making authority is considered as it operates under these four alternative, but in important respects overlapping, forms or constructs used in studying and practicing American federalism. Since the exposition of the models is couched primarily in terms of issues relevant to the distribution of administrative discretion, the chapter focuses more on the implications of the models for executive leadership than on the substance of particular public policies.

The conceptions used in this discussion of federalism and administrative discretion are dual federalism, cooperative federalism, what will be identified here as national federalism, and the two versions of new federalism promulgated by Presidents Richard Nixon and Ronald Reagan. These models are offered in roughly chronological fashion. I must emphasize, however, that no conception of intergovernmental relations ever prevails to the exclusion of all others. Indeed, different patterns or models of intergovernmental relations, allowing for varying degrees of administrative discretion and opportunities for leadership, will prevail among different agencies at the same time and perhaps even within the same "holding company" agency.

It is apparent that models serve important functions for actors in intergovernmental relations. For example, they suggest, and in some cases demand, particular courses of action when particular problems arise. The adjectival paradigms (dual, cooperative, new, and so on) influence both the policy content and the procedures employed by generalists and specialists in the public sector. Especially in the case of administrators, models aid in coping with ambiguous decision situations. After the four informal models of federalism are examined, with a focus on their implications for administrative discretion, it should be apparent what some of the other functions are. Each of the conceptualizations is examined in terms of its relevance to several aspects of executive leadership. I am attempting to elucidate the following issues with the presentation of the dual, cooperative, national, and new federalism constructs: (1) the implications of the models for the distribution of discretion among federal, state, and local administrators, specifically for the ability of federal administrators to dominate state and local administrators, and for state ability to dominate local administration; (2) the impact of the models on the role of bureaucrats as a group in the public policy process, especially in the effects of the models on the power relationships of specialist administrators and state and local elected officials and on the ways in which the perceptions of administrators influence their use of discretion; and (3) the openness of the models themselves to the consideration of these and other significant intergovernmental and managerial issues.

Dual Federalism

Whether or not it described in sufficiently accurate terms the nature of the American intergovernmental system before the New Deal, the concept of dual federalism was and is nevertheless a useful analytic device for testing hypotheses about the relation between models of federalism and administrative discretion.

The U.S. Supreme Court frequently in the nineteenth century and until the 1930s endorsed the view, also supported by most presidents, that the national government and the states constituted distinct sovereignties. Their administrative and other powers were to be exercised separately and independently. For example, in the 1876 case of *U.S.* v. *Cruikshank* (92 U.S. 542) the Court said that federal and state authorities are different: "The powers which one possesses, the other does not. They are established for different purposes, and have separate jurisdictions." By 1940, however, dual federalism, associated with maximum state independence and discretion, seemed to have been abandoned for good. President Franklin D. Roosevelt had a different view of federalism, and the New Deal–dominated Supreme Court took the position that the judiciary should no longer attempt to impose its own views of social and economic policy on the administrative and legislative branches of the national government. Dual federalism was viewed essentially as a mechanism for the implementation of conservative political values.

Dual federalism, including some of its administrative aspects, is still occasionally encountered, however. For example, the Supreme Court, under President Nixon's choice for chief justice, Warren Burger, generally declined to enjoin state proceedings in the criminal justice area because of the separation that was supposed to exist between the federal and state administrative establishments. According to a revived dual federalism, governors and other state officials had the privilege—and obligation—of enforcing their own laws in their own administrative and judicial institutions. Thus federal judges normally would not be expected to consider charges made against state administrative officials when federal review of their activities would clearly amount to interference. What Louise Weinberg identifies as the new judicial federalism, the advent of which was signaled by Nixon's appointment of Burger as chief justice, "requir[ed] deferences to state administration . . . that [previously] were thought unnecessary or unwise" (1977:1192–94). In the 1971 case of *Younger* v. *Harris* (401 U.S. 37), Justice Hugo Black urged upon federal officials the need to recognize that "the entire country is made up of a union of separate state governments." In Black's judgment, "the National government would fare best if the States and their institutions [were] left free to perform their separate functions in their separate ways" (401 U.S. 44).

President Nixon's general revenue-sharing program, which was in effect for only a relatively short period (1972–86), was also consistent with dual federalism because it allowed recipients maximum discretion in the use of funds granted and encouraged the maintenance of separate national and state-local policy arenas. Revenue sharing was designed in part to bolster the independent decision-making capabilities of state and local governments. Block grants, which were successfully pushed in the first Reagan term, are also complementary with traditional federalism because they implicitly recognize, even if not as strongly as revenue sharing, that state and local administrators are not the mere functionaries of Washington. One of the traditional justifications for federalism is that multiple centers of power and, hence, discretion will encourage leadership to develop more prolifically than will the deadening hand of centralization. Revenue sharing and block grants should be contrasted with other aid approaches which may be viewed as seeking to bring Washington and state-local goverments into lockstep alignment.

The concept of dual federalism serves to restrain federal attempts to dominate the personnel and activities of state and local governments. With the decline of the old dual federalism, the primary barriers to federal efforts to direct these governments, and particularly their administrative establishments, became essentially federal attitudes about appropriate and inappropriate control procedures. Dual federalism, in contrast, presupposes the equality of state bureaucrats with federal bureaucrats because, in their proper realms, both state and federal governments are sovereign and therefore equal (adapted from Corwin, 1950).

In the dual federalism model it is possible and desirable to categorize public functions into federal and state. This the U.S. Constitution presumably did. The states develop their own apportionments of functions with the local governments they create. Dual federalism offers the opportunity for state governments to coordinate fully all public functions within the state because program direction is not fragmented among state and multiple federal authorities. Any shifts of power between governmental systems which occur are made without reference to their impacts on administrative discretion within particular policy arenas. Dual federalism focuses on systemwide patterns of interaction between the federal and state governments. Any substantial return now to conceptualizations of dual federalism would, however, redistribute administrative discretion. Whether avowedly or not, it would constitute a reaction to the cooperative and national models which are explicated in this chapter.

Dual federalism constituted no threat to the power of governors and other state and local elected officials over function-oriented administrators at these levels. Whichever dominated in a particular situation—the generalists or the specialists—would depend on the legal and political resources each was able to muster. The federal government would not intervene in behalf of either side. The weight of law and tradition, of course, would mainly support state generalists. Dual federalism does not imply a theme of hostility in the relations between administrative specialists and political generalists, but state and local administrators probably would resent being cut off from regular interaction with specialists employed by the federal government, and this resentment likely would be directed toward their generalist superiors.

Dual federalism presupposes a limited range of bureaucratic concerns. The national government as a whole, under this concept, may become involved in only a small number of domestic activities. This was frequently stressed in the 1980s by Reagan administration spokespersons. In the dual federalism model it is the state governments which have almost sole responsibility to provide leadership to promote the public health, safety, and good order (Corwin in McCloskey, 1962:200–201). According to the pure model of dual federalism, as revived by Reagan's attorney general, Edwin Meese, national power cannot be extended through judicial reinterpretation, even though problems have arisen which were not anticipated by the Framers of the Constitution. But when state and local political systems will not provide leadership and their administrative systems cannot respond to nationally perceived citizen needs, a model supporting governmental separatism loses support. When state and local political discretion is employed to repress the legitimate aspirations of people and to discriminate in the provision of public services, the notion that national and state operations should flow along like parallel but separate streams is intolerable.

Yet, despite its defects from a practical standpoint, dual federalism is conceptually perhaps the clearest of the models whose implications for executive leadership are assessed in this chapter. Nevertheless, it responds negatively to most significant intergovernmental and managerial issues because it assumes a fixed distribution of governmental power and rejects ongoing interaction among national, state, and local officials in the public policy process. The dual federalism conception assumes the impossibility of administrators from more than one governmental level working together harmoniously because the relationship between the federal government and state governments will almost inevitably be tense and noncollaborative.

Cooperative Federalism

The cooperative conception of American federalism is generally defined as one in which the central government and the state governments, using whatever powers they are legally, politically, and technically capable of exercising, work together, collectively employing the leadership patterns suggested by the problems they are trying to solve on behalf of the American people, who are, simultaneously, citizens of states and of the nation. Customarily, cooperative federalism denotes national assistance to states and localities to respond to needs which are felt there but which the subnational governments have inadequate resources to cope with, particularly with regard to finances but also professional leadership capabilities.

It is, therefore, the usual interpretation of cooperative federalism that a wide sharing of functions obtains among federal, state, and local governments. The crucial question with dual federalism—which set of agencies, federal, state, or local, has jurisdiction in which areas—is no longer very important. Instead, the emphasis is on the most potent combination of authorities to provide the leadership to solve widely perceived social and economic problems. Cooperative federalism deemphasizes the importance of "proper" governmental roles. It is obvious that the national government's range of functions has been growing. States and localities, however, still constitute semiautonomous centers of power which prevent the transformation of the United States from a federal into a unitary system of government totally dominated from Washington.

Early cooperative federalism was mostly consistent with the belief that government in a country as vast as the United States is more responsive when states and localities constitute semiautonomous centers of leadership. In state-local administrative relations, it did not (as practiced, for example, in the Woodrow Wilson years) pose a major threat to the original notions of a bipartite federal system rather than a tripartite system. Most federal aid was directed to state government functions, particularly to serve rural needs (e.g., roads), and such aid as was extended to urban areas generally was channeled through state agencies. It encouraged the recipient governments to provide leadership in solving problems that were important to them. As cooperative federalism continued to develop, however, especially in the Truman administration, direct federal-local administrative relations became more common and the state frequently had no significant leadership role, simply giving a pro forma consent to programs in which it had no major ongoing responsibilities (e.g., public housing).

Any shift of power between governmental levels while cooperative federalism is the working model would affect administrative discretion. The bureaucratic role is much enhanced in cooperative federalism as compared with dual federalism. The bureaucrats are the brains of cooperative federalism. Such cooperative activities as go on in the American intergovernmental system go on mostly among bureaucrats, not on so extensive a basis among national and state and local legislators or elected executives.

Cooperative federalism is a model of fragmentation. National, state, and local administrative agencies are bound together not on a governmentwide but on a functional basis. There is leadership within but not over the large number of policy arenas in which modern governments are active. To some critics cooperative federalism became dysfunctional as programmatic ties between national and state and local administrators were strengthened by the accelerating growth in fiscal, technical, professional, and other links between governments. Many programs of cooperative federalism were supportive of what Deil Wright has labeled "a hodgepodge of independent professional and functional fiefdoms" (1978:211). In degenerative cooperative federalism, policy formulation tends to be aggregative rather than distributive. That is, it represents the summation of the policy orientations of each discrete set of administrative agencies and its leaders. The role of generalists, most notably elected officials, is weak.

In this conceptualization, executives, whether federal, state, or local, would logically see themselves as members of problem-solving teams within rather narrow functional areas. With regard to the issue of domination, therefore, it is not necessarily assumed that federal administrators will have a role that always stands out over and above the roles of state and local officials in their cooperative activities. Because of growing federal fiscal dominance, however, the federal government, through an evolving grant system, did come more and more to employ state and local administrative agencies as executors of nationally defined policy, rather than primarily aiding in the solution of subnationally determined needs. Even so, different federal grants provide for different amounts of subnational discretion. And even with fairly specific categorical grants, if the recipient governments can spend the money they receive essentially for whatever they desire, despite what the regulations say (this is the "fungibility" problem), de facto they have discretion no matter what the espoused theory of intergovernmental relations may be. Realistically, the larger and more complex a federal program is, the harder it may be for the feds to exercise control over state and local leaders. To get what they want, most federal administrators may have to bargain away lower-priority objectives.

The pure cooperative model, like the dual federalism conception, thus represents a considerably fictionalized picture of how the American federal system works on a day-to-day basis. Cooperation and conflict have, of course, always existed. Cooperative federalism, or at least some manifestations of it, has operated in the United States since the beginning of the republic. But despite its long tradition, the cooperative federalism model may not be very open to the consideration of significant intergovernmental and managerial issues. In its most recent expressions the emphasis has been too much directed toward problem-solving activities within narrow, substantially autonomous bureaucratic categories.

National Federalism

The image of the American federal system according to national federalism is that of a pin—Washington—with many shafts extending outward from it representing essentially equal state governments, counties, cities, areawide and nonprofit agencies, and so on ("pinwheel federalism"). All revolve around Washington (Weissert, 1980:19). The greatest amount of discretion, including administrative discretion, lies with national leaders, especially the president, so that problem-solving activities (the focus of national as well as cooperative federalism) aimed at helping the nation as a whole can be consistently and effectively articulated. This model is consistent with standard public administrative dogma, which holds that achieving efficiency and maintaining necessary control require centralization and minimal "field" discretion. This sets up an obvious conflict with the tenets of traditional federalism. National federalism's proponents, according to Vincent Ostrom, a critic of what I am describing here, anticipate "the final burial of the traditional doctrines of American federalism and the development of a new 'model'" to make federalism a positive instead of a negative political force (Ostrom, 1976:26, citing Sundquist, 1969). Ostrom's primary target was the administrative ideology he saw as dominant during the Lyndon Johnson creative federalism years. Executive officials are usually seen as the principal forces behind national federalism, but the real "villains," if we may identify them as such for discussion purposes, may not be the administration but members of Congress playing state legislator or city councilperson-at-large, designing increasingly specific programs both to aid the constituencies they represent and to ensure that credit for federal largesse is unmistakably assignable.

National federalism denotes less of a genuine federal-state-local partnership than does cooperative federalism. In the national federalism conception, policy is formulated at the national level (with the president at the apex of the policy pyramid) and subnational executives are given varying amounts of responsibility for implementing it. Therefore, how much leadership subnational executives are able to exercise is determined by actors at the federal level. In national federalism, state and local administrative agencies can be compared to the middle and lower ranks of a corporate bureaucracy. The president is truly the chief executive. The idea that these subordinate ranks should have independent policies of their own is strongly discouraged. They are paid well (e.g., grants), the argument goes, and should follow orders. Such decentralization as may be needed in a particular problem area will be put into effect, not on account of any antifederal bias, but strictly because it is the most desirable administrative strategy. Federal administrators will employ grant programs with their financial incentives and regulations to coerce (if necessary) the subnational recipients to behave as Washington deems appropriate. Project grants allow for the least discretion for state and local administrators and, consequently, least encourage the development of independent leadership initiatives below the federal level.

The more specific grants are, the fewer opportunities there will be for the exercise of leadership when situations not anticipated in federally promulgated guidelines arise. Responses typically are programmed rather than spontaneous. Leadership, wise or unwise, imaginative or rigidly conservative, falls mostly to federal rather than state and local officials. If state and local executives exercise leadership, it will be in spite of rather than because of Washington. Leadership may have to be camouflaged. Deceptive practices may be required to mislead federal officials concerning what is actually going on outside the Capitol.

Direct federal-local ties become even more important in the application of the national federalism model than with cooperative federalism. When Lyndon Johnson's creative federalism was the expression of national federalism ideas in the 1960s, Roscoe Martin, along with Coleman Ransone for many years a member of the political science faculty at the University of Alabama, argued that there was no longer any reason for any jurisdiction, particularly a city, to have to do without the knowledge, imagination, and perspective required for creative problem solving. The nationalization of these resources, he contended, rivaled in importance the nationalization of fiscal resources, which was first taken advantage of in a massive way in the cooperative federalism of the Franklin D. Roosevelt years (Martin, 1965).

Recent shortfalls in federal resources have not been accompanied by a lessening of federal efforts to reduce the discretion of state and local officials. Indeed, it seems that as the size of the federal carrot has been shrinking the federal stick has been getting larger. Control, whether exercised through grants or regulations, is still control, and it is inversely related to opportunities for state and local administrators to exercise independent leadership. Regulatory national federalism is even less consistent with traditional federalism than the more penetrating forms of cooperative federalism. Of course, the justification for regulatory federalism—the expression itself may be a contradiction in terms—is that the problems requiring intrusive federal regulatory initiatives respect no jurisdictional boundaries. Following this line of reasoning, it is problems that determine the degree of centralization or decentralization. Notions of federalism may only get in the way of rational solutions. Problems necessitate certain administrative arrangements, and these may not permit much in the way of discretion—and hence leadership opportunities—for state and local leaders.

In most respects, national federalism, like cooperative federalism, is favorable toward the power of public executives as a group. Most of the benefits accrue to national bureaucrats, however. A professional leadership elite, most evident in the federal administrative establishment, guides in the development of new programs. Members of this elite may not be especially concerned about national prerogatives for their own sake. Their primary concerns typically are policy-oriented. They are interested in the implementation of programs and program arrangements that have the backing of solid empirical research. Also like cooperative federalism, national federalism capitalizes on the propensity of professional administrators to collaborate (even if not on an equal basis) irrespective of the governmental jurisdictions they happen to work for in behalf of policy aims indicated by the specialized training and experience they share.

Because of the professional and technical orientation of national federalism, the governance of specialist administrators by amateur state and local elected officials is made much more difficult. As with cooperative federalism, and even more so, the leadership role of elected officials is likely to be weak. Political values, according to this model, are supposed to be subordinated to rationalism and empiricism in the public policy process. National federalism recognizes the possibility of long-term shifts of power between governments in only one direction—toward the national government. As state and local executive professionalism increases, however, it can be expected that national executives may be able increasingly to delegate some important policy implementation responsibilities down the hierarchy. In this respect, shifts of power between governments would affect, and affect most, administrative discretion. Nevertheless, state and local executives, operating with a national federalism perspective, could not help but perceive their essentially inferior position. Any shift of power simply to benefit the states or to fortify their constitutional position in the American Union is out of the question.

National federalism is open to the consideration of important intergovernmental and managerial issues, even if it is characterized by an inherently pro-federal bias. If it can be shown empirically that changes in existing ways of operating are in some way defective, or not as productive as they could be, the national federalist would be willing to make the needed changes.

New Federalism

Finally, I will examine the new federalisms of Presidents Richard Nixon and Ronald Reagan with a view toward identifying their implications for administrative discretion. President Nixon, in launching his new federalism initiative in 1969, the centerpiece of which was revenue sharing, said that his main idea was to shift power and financial resources to the governments closest to the people. A member of the staff that worked out the details of the program, William Safire, said that Nixon's new federalism amounted to "national goals [being] set at the national level by the Congress and the president with localities making decisions about how this national policy was to be carried out" (Safire, 1982).

President Reagan's new federalism, which contemplated turning back to the states numerous programs for which the federal government currently has principal responsibility, along with some federal financial support for a limited period, was presumably directed even more toward a return to state executives of the discretion which, in the Reagan view, had been usurped by the federal government. In launching his ambitious new federalism initiative, President Reagan contended in 1981 that "in a single stroke we will be accomplishing a realignment that will end cumbersome administration and spiraling costs at the Federal level while we insure these programs will be more responsive to both the people they are meant to help and the people who pay for them" ("Text of President's Message to the Nation," *New York Times*, 1982:A16).

In thinking reminiscent of early cooperative federalism, the rhetoric of Reagan's new federalism was to the effect that Washington would henceforth be a partner, but only a partner, with state and local governments in wrestling with some of the more difficult problems that had to be handled by government. But the most desperate need was for more authority and responsibility—what discretion means fundamentally—to be given back to the states. Upon close examination, Reagan's new federalism is seen to represent a sharper break from cooperative and national federalism than Nixon's new federalism. As far as the state-local relationship was concerned, Reagan's new federalism took the position that state and local officials did not have to continue as rivals, particularly if federal intrusiveness, which had disturbed traditional patterns of state-local contacts, ceased. Without federal "help," state and local officials, both generalists and specialists, would presumably work well together.

The shift of power contemplated in both Nixon's and Reagan's new federalisms was designed to affect administrative discretion. It was intended that more responsibility would be put in the hands of political generalists, who, presumably, would be able to keep a closer rein on administrative specialists once the heavy-handed federal interference was removed.

A 1980 retrospective view of Nixonian new federalism said that two of its major goals were to "reduce the size of the [federal] bureaucracy" and to "simplify administrative machinery" ("The Overloaded System," *National Civic Review*, 1980:304, 306). These objectives, if operationalized, should have provided more discretion for state and possibly local executives, even if the ultimate beneficiaries were supposed to be elected officials at those levels. The federal bureaucracy would have less scope, less muscle, and hence less ability to direct state and local executives, whether specialists or generalists. Reagan's new federalism assumed that the states wanted to and could assume larger roles in the administration and funding of essential social programs. It stressed that Washington, and especially its bureaucrats, did not have all the wisdom about how best to design and implement substantive and procedural reforms. It emphasized that state and local officials, particularly general government executives and legislators, were better able than those in Washington to perceive and respond to grass-roots needs.

The new federalism of both Nixon and Reagan sought to weaken administrative power by scattering the professional, technical, fiscal, and other resources under bureaucratic control between the federal government and state and local governments, connected henceforth by looser ties than those represented in narrowly focused project grants and cross-cutting regulations. In the new federalisms, administrative agencies are to be tightly controlled by the chief generalists, the elected officials. Thus policy formulation within a particular governmental arena would be an essentially distributive rather than a merely aggregative process. Decisions would be made from the top within each level of government rather than simply being added up on the basis of choices made by virtually independent administrative agencies. Both new federalisms reflect an emphasis on governmental jurisdictions as a whole rather than specific administrative functions. The new federalisms, in their most positive interpretations, also reflect the belief that all public functions cannot be shared among all governments, that structural spaces between federal administration and state and local administration should be observed, and that, most important, the constitutional divisions of functions among American governments, made in the late eighteenth century, still have relevance late in the twentieth century.

Of course, as Herbert Kaufman (1960) showed, when functionally specialized personnel share similar outlooks because they have similar educational backgrounds and patterns of professional socialization, formal regulations that seek to limit the exercise of discretion within a policy system may not be necessary. The decisions made by leaders, at whatever level of responsibility, will be fairly predictable based on the professional norms to which they have become increasingly committed over a long period of time. This finding, by implication, tends to diminish the significance of some of the more recent presidential decentralization efforts discussed here.

The asserted tenets of the new federalisms had inevitably to cloud the perceptions particularly of local executives. They supposedly were to receive more direction from state executives and less from Washington specialists. Yet state officials may not have the ability or interest to give coherent direction to complex urban administrative programs. Also, the rhetoric of new federalism, whether of President Nixon or President Reagan, exceeded the substance. As we have seen, in many respects subnational administrators are subject to more Washington regulations than ever. One could, therefore, have expected considerable administrative schizophrenia when presidential words stressed a restored power position while administrative activity at the state and local levels continued to be heavily influenced by decisions made mostly in Washington.

Both new federalisms are open to the consideration of significant intergovernmental and managerial issues. The new federalism of Nixon underlined managerial issues more, the Reagan thrust a revival of a lost state constitutional position. Each of these two, like national federalism, reflects broader systemic concerns than does cooperative federalism, which, ironically in view of its popularity as an interpretation of the American federal system, is probably the least useful of the four as an analytic device.

Conclusion

It should be emphasized that in the American intergovernmental system problems are generally addressed by both generalists and specialists within government and, of equal importance, by interest groups outside formal structures without conscious reference to presidentially defined models of federalism or any others. Even though a particular conception of federalism may not be regarded as binding, however, it is not, as we have seen, without effect. These models either directly or indirectly condition the position, power, and activities of federal, state, and local executives and the administrative institutions they direct. For these reasons they warrant more study from the perspective of their impact on executive leadership than they have heretofore received.

Although no precisely cyclical succession of models of federalism can readily be identified, it is obvious that American intergovernmental relationships undergo continuous change and that some of these changes are recurring. It is also undeniable that the president continues potentially to be an important agent of change in the American federal system. Elements both of conflict and cooperation, dominance and submission, always may be discerned within governments as well as between them. Not only will one model, therefore, overlap with another at a particular time, but the models presented here, variations on them, or perhaps different conceptualizations, will find contrasting applications in different and sometimes even in the same policy arenas. This chapter, however, has identified some important themes applicable across the policy spectrum. It is to issues such as these that students and practitioners of executive leadership in the public sector must pay particular attention if they are to understand and work with the complexities of American federalism.

7 GUBERNATORIAL LEADERSHIP AND STATE ADMINISTRATION: INSTITUTIONAL ORIENTATIONS IN A CHANGING POLITICAL ENVIRONMENT

Cheryl M. Miller and Deil S. Wright

The roles and relationships of administrative agencies in the American political system are problematic and controversial, to say the least. From an external, public, or citizen's standpoint, the opinions about administrative agencies (public bureaucracies) commonly cluster around two contrasting attitudinal poles. At one extreme are public perceptions of powerful, impersonal, insensitive leviathans running roughshod over citizens, clients, and even their ostensible political superiors—elected executives, legislators, and courts. At the other extreme is the idea that administrative agencies are weak, unimaginative, uninspired "wimps" that need to be goaded, herded, or otherwise pushed into proper or effective performance (Knott and Miller, 1987).

These externally identified polar perceptions also have their internally located counterparts. Anthony Downs (1967), for example, suggests that administrative agencies, "bureaus" is his term, fluctuate between two extremes when attempting to control and cope with changes affecting their policy space or turf(s). At one extreme is the "superman syndrome," which might be summarized by the phrase, "Anything you can do, we can do better!" At the other end of the spectrum is Downs's "shrinking violet" viewpoint. This might be likened to the biblical parable of the person given only one talent, which was promptly buried in the ground for safekeeping.

There may be administrative agencies whose actions, policies, roles, and relationships come close to fitting one or more of these external- and internal-defined categories. For the vast majority of public agencies, however, these categories are stereotypes that match almost none of the real-world patterns involving power, purpose, process, and performance of public sector administration. Dispelling these myths or caricatures, however, does little to address and answer important questions about the role and functioning of public bureaucracy within the vast middle range(s) between these extremes.

In turning toward a positive formulation of significant questions about bureaucracy in the American political system, our attention, like that of many others, gravitates toward the relationship between chief executives and administrative agencies. Executive influence over and direction of administrative agencies has been a central issue throughout two centuries of U.S. political, legal, and administrative history. Its prominence and association with the administrative reform movement is the subject of a recent book-length analysis (Knott and Miller, 1987). Executive control has escalated in significance in recent decades for a host of reasons, not the least of which has been the enormous growth in size and confirmed influence of administrative agencies.

Approaches to the study of executive-administrative relations have been numerous, varied, selective, and eclectic. To the extent that research has clustered on some topics more than others, it is our view that studies of national (presidential) and local (mayor or manager) administrative guidance have far exceeded the attention devoted to executive-administrative relations at the state level. Among the few scholars who gave deliberate and sustained analysis to this topic at the state level, the name of Coleman B. Ransone stands out. In his early and major book on the office of the governor, Ransone (1956) raised explicitly and prominently the function of management/administration as a significant problem faced by chief executives.

That systematic research on executive-administrative relationships came

Table 7.1. Numbers of Full-Time-Equivalent National and State Government Employees (in millions)

Year	National	States
1951	2.6	0.9
1955	2.4	1.1
1960	2.4	1.4
1965	2.5	1.8
1970	2.9	2.3
1975	2.8	3.1
1980	2.8	3.1
1985	2.9	3.3
1989	2.9	3.6

Source: U.S. Bureau of the Census, 1990.

somewhat late to state government is not surprising. That it remains in a distinctly subordinate status is more surprising. Several features of state-level institutional shifts argue for the appropriateness of increased and sustained research on state administration and especially on its status in relation to executive (as well as legislative) oversight and influence. In this chapter we explore those institutional features.

What have been the chief changes in the character, content, and context of state administration over the past three decades—decades that coincidentally spanned a major segment of Coleman Ransone's research? At the risk of some oversimplification, but in keeping with our institutional focus, we note shifts in three areas: the overall growth of the state administrative establishment, changes in the office of the governor, and the resurgence of state legislatures.

State Administration

Size

Growth of the state-level bureaucracy is occasionally noted but rarely publicized. Indeed, political and public rhetoric feature attacks on the large federal (national) bureaucracy. They leave the impression that the size of the national administrative establishment has outstripped (and even displaced) state administrative operations. In fact, the opposite has occurred.

Table 7.1 lists figures (in millions) for the number of full-time-equivalent (FTE) employees in the national government and the total for the fifty state governments. Civilian employment levels in the national government have remained within a relatively stable range, from 2.4 to 2.9 million during the past four decades. In contrast, the state administrative establishment has grown both rapidly and constantly since the 1950s.

During much of the 1960s and well into the 1970s, the average annual growth rate of state employment (FTE) was around 5 percent. There are numerous and varied explanations for this trend (Chubb, 1985), but those factors lie outside our present focus. The central point is that the state administrative establishment, although divided into fifty separate political entities, is the largest aggregate bureaucratic entity in the United States. Its size alone justifies attention to its development and direction.

Depth and Diversity

Aggregate growth and current size can be supplemented with data on scope and diversity as factors compelling a focus on state bureaucracy. The fourfold rise in the total number of state employees across four decades could have occurred entirely within the existing departments and agencies of state government. This might be construed as administrative growth in depth. A large measure of such growth did occur in standard, "old-line" state agencies such as higher education, highways, health, and welfare. But growth in depth has been only a partial and perhaps not the most significant feature of state-level bureaucratic change. Much more dramatic has been growth in the variety of types or diversity of state agencies.

The expanded diversity of state administration can be documented by counting the number of states that had different types of administrative agencies over various time periods since the 1950s. Table 7.2 provides information resulting from extensive tallying from the *Book of the States* (biennial supplements on administrative agencies by function) (Haas and Wright, 1989). The top section (I) lists the titles of a large number of agencies that have existed in forty-five or more states since the 1950s. These agencies might be viewed as the common and long-term core of the state bureaucracy.

The other sections of the table indicate agencies that were created in a lesser number of states in the 1960s and 1970s. The titles of the various agencies in these sections indicate that an increasing number of states moved administratively into more and more fields of activity. Stated simply and succinctly, Table 7.2 shows the enlarged diversity of state government. The array of agencies listed in the different sections of the table also conveys a sense of the immense scope of activities that are found within state administration.

The creation of new and the expansion of old state agencies is in several respects the untold story of public administrative growth in the United States over recent decades. That complete story cannot be related here. What can be highlighted, however, are issues involving the important political and policy relationships of this expanded bureaucracy to the institutions of democratic control—the governor and legislature. Before focusing on those issues and relationships, however, we need to recognize the changing intergovernmental context in which state administration is embedded.

Impacts of Federal Aid

Two sets of figures can be used as general and somewhat superficial indicators of the changing patterns of intergovernmental relations as they affect state administration. One series is the proportion of state agencies (or agency heads) reporting the receipt of federal aid; the second set records the percentage of state agencies that secure 50 percent or more of their respec-

Table 7.2. Proliferation of State Agencies, 1959–1985

I. 1959–1985: Agencies that existed in 45 or more states

Adjutant General	Advertising (Tourism)	Aging
Agriculture	Air Pollution	Attorney General
Auditor	Banking	Budget
Civil Defense	Corrections	Education
Employment Security	Fishing	Food and Drugs
Forestry	Geology	Health
Higher Education	Highway Patrol	Highways
Insurance	Labor	Library
Library (Law)	Liquor Control	Mental Health
Motor Vehicles	Parks	Parole
Public Assistance	Public Utilities	Purchasing
Secretary of State	Securities	Soil Conservation
Taxation	Treasurer	Vocational Education
Water Pollution	Water Resources	Welfare
Workers' Compensation		

II. 1965–1985: Agencies that existed in 35 or more states

Administration/Finance	Aeronautics	Commerce
Comptroller	Economic Development	Federal Relations
Labor Arbitration	Natural Resources	Oil and Gas
Personnel	Planning	

III. 1971–1985: Agencies that existed in 35 or more states

Air Pollution	Community Affairs	Court Administration
Criminal Justice	Drug Abuse	Economic Opportunity
Human Resources	Information	Juvenile Delinquency

IV. 1975–1985: Agencies that existed in 25 or more states

Arts	Consumer Protection	Energy
Environment	Ethics	Housing Finance
Manpower	Mass Transportation	Medicaid
Mental Retardation	Occupational Health and Safety	Occupational Licensing
Railroads	Vocational Rehabilitation	

Table 7.3. Proportion of State Agencies Receiving Federal Aid

Year	Number of Agencies	Receipt of Federal Aid	Dependent on Federal Aid for over 50 Percent of Budget
1964	877	33	10
1968	904	53	15
1974	745	59	15
1978	505	71	16
1984	449	59	14

Source: Wright, 1990.

tive budgets from federal aid sources. The relevant figures are shown in Table 7.3 and are derived from recurrent questionnaire surveys of state agency heads by the American State Administrators Project (ASAP) (Wright, 1990).

The rise and decline of federal aid, in relative terms, is reflected in the rise and fall (between 1978 and 1984) of the proportions. It is not simply the changes or trends in the figures that warrant special emphasis, however. More pertinent and significant are the impacts of federal aid and its receipt on executive leadership and administrative accountability.

Two further questions asked of state agency heads are relevant to the accountability issue. One involves state-level oversight (by the governor and legislature) of the federally funded activities. The second centers on the nationally imposed constraints, limits, or "strings" attached to federal aid funds. The figures in Table 7.4 constitute rough indicators of state-level administrative autonomy encouraged by federal aid and the level of unease among administrators with the limits attached to use of federal funds, that is, the proportions of agency heads who would use the money differently if the national constraints were removed.

The level of reported administrative autonomy resulting from federal aid remained relatively constant from the 1960s to the 1980s. Roughly half of the agency heads on the receiving end of federal funds indicated that they enjoyed less oversight from the governor and legislature as a result of receiving federal aid. This degree of perceived discretion clearly poses problems for coordinated and controlled administrative operations in state government. The accountability issue is only one of several that seem likely to arise as a result of administrative autonomy.

A counterpoint to state-level autonomy is the degree of national-level constraint imposed on state administrative discretion by the acceptance of federal aid. A surrogate and subjective measure of the impact of national limitations is the proportion of state agency heads who would prefer to spend the federal funds differently. The percentage of "reallocators" has undergone significant shifts over the past three decades. Administrators who would alter the use of federal funds constituted slightly over half of the aid recipients in the 1960s. The proportion escalated to about three-fourths in the 1970s before dropping to two-thirds in the 1980s.

A substantial majority of state administrators holds views on program funding priorities which are at variance with those that accompany the receipt and use of federal aid. A crucial question, which cannot be pursued here, is whether those administrators' preferences are responsive to or even directly consistent with the priorities set by the governor, legislature, or both. The question, however, emphasizes the need to describe and assess the changing roles of these two institutional entities.

Office of the Governor

From Figurehead to Executive Leader

The transformation of the American governorship has occupied the interests of numerous foreign and American scholars. A wealth of descriptive, prescriptive, and normative literature can be found on the office of governor. It has been studied on a state-specific level, comparatively, and with an eye to isolating aggregate general and temporal trends (Lipson, 1939; Beyle and Williams, 1972; Sabato, 1983).

Two early landmark treatments of the evolution of the office are Lipson's

Table 7.4. Federal Aid and Administrative Autonomy

Year	Number of Agencies	Federal Aid Leads to Less State-Level Oversight	Would Use (Reallocate) Federal Funds Differently if National Restrictions Were Removed
1964	877	50	54
1968	904	45	58
1974	745	49	75
1978	505	50	73
1984	449	57	67

Source: Wright, 1990.

(1939) classic study and Ransone's (1956) comparative volume. A prominent theme found in these studies, as well as in other, more recent analyses of gubernatorial power, is the importance of gubernatorial control over state administration. Lipson noted that Progressive Movement reforms such as reorganization, the short ballot, and the executive budget made "the administrative work of state governments better planned than before, and the credit rests with the governor's new-found executive leadership" (Lipson, 1939:246). Similarly, Ransone concluded his twenty-five-state survey with the observation that a fragmented administrative establishment "results in an irresponsible executive branch which is not subject to the control of either the governor, the legislature, or the people" (Ransone, 1956:385). For Ransone, the remedy lay in "consolidating the executive branch into a relatively small number of single-headed departments subject to gubernatorial control" (1956:382).

Both authors concluded that the executive function had grown into analytically distinct parts. Lipson observed that the governor was both the chief executive and the chief legislator and served a vital policy leadership function. According to Ransone, the governor wore three hats: chief of party, legislative leader, and chief administrator. These hats helped the governor perform three noteworthy functions in the areas of policy formation, public relations, and management. Ransone found the public relations role to be the most time-consuming, the policy formation role the most significant ("like a thread through all the governor's other functions"), and the management role third in both time and significance (1956:147).

In an update of his initial study, Ransone (1982) found that in the 1970s the three gubernatorial roles were still descriptive of how governors spent their time. Public relations remained the most time-consuming function (at 37 percent), and policy formation was still the most significant one. There was, however, "a shift in the 1970s in the direction of a greater emphasis on management," with governors spending more time on it (29 percent) and according it more importance (1982:97). On the basis of these findings, Ransone speculated that the governor may have become "more an administrator than a policymaker" (1982:162). This statement closely parallels the more detailed, administrator-based survey finding of Glenn Abney and Thomas P. Lauth that "governors appear to be inclined to seek to be managers rather than policy leaders" (1983:49).

Staff Capabilities

Adequate staff appears to be a necessary but not sufficient condition aiding the governor in the functions of policy formation, public relations, and management. Ransone was one of the earliest observers to note that gubernatorial staffing patterns and formal powers "do make a difference in his [the governor's] ability to set public policy" (1956:362). Staff size was inadequate, according to Ransone, in the twenty-five states covered in his earlier study. In his later assessment, Ransone found significant increases in staff size, quality, and specialization. There were, for example, staff assistants for five common functions in all the states: executive assistant, legislative liaison, legal counsel, press secretary, and appointments secretary (Ransone, 1982:109–10). Thad L. Beyle supplemented these findings with a 1979 survey, which disclosed that half the states had at least one gubernatorial staffer involved in policy development functions (Beyle and Muchmore, 1983:162). According to Ransone, one certainty is that gubernatorial "staff members play a substantial role in policy determination if for no other reason than the fact they are in constant touch with the governor" (1982:132).

The quality and the experience of the staff are also important. Gubernatorial staff tend to have political backgrounds, are recruited largely on the basis of a personal relationship with the governor or his political party, and operate in a highly charged, political force field. Donald P. Sprengel (1972) confirmed that gubernatorial staff were similar to other political elites, had extensive political experience, and usually had prior links with the governor. A politicized staff, operating in a politically charged environment, may not always reflect well on the governor, however. Alan J. Wyner (1972) found a high degree of dissatisfaction with gubernatorial staff among "outsiders" like statehouse office personnel, journalists, and lobbyists. He attributed the negative staff image to the fallout caused by unpopular decisions the staff make affecting these outsiders. Contemporary governors may possess better staff than ever before, but they are advised to be vigilant in choosing persons who will avoid protectiveness, gatekeeping, and groupthink tendencies.

Formal Powers

Early state constitutions provided few formal powers to the governor and produced "executive enfeeblement" (Sabato, 1983:4). More recently there has been a shift to "executive empowerment." Beyle and Lynn R. Muchmore (1983) cite three changes between 1955 and 1980 which have given governors more potential power than previously. First, the number of governors allowed four-year terms increased from twenty-nine to forty-six. This, they contend, enables governors to spend less time on reelection politics and more on policy and administration. Second, forty-seven rather than forty-two states granted the governor sole budget-making authority. Third, the number of governors who could succeed themselves increased from six to twenty-three.

Joseph A. Schlesinger (1965) was one of the first scholars to explore the relationship between formal powers and the governor's ability to influence state administration. His index of formal powers was based on criteria involving the budget, appointive and veto powers, and tenure potential. Modernized state constitutions and statutes give governors more powers than ever before. Based on his 1965 index, Schlesinger rated none of the states as having a strong governor and judged ten as having very weak governors. Beyle's update for the 1980s of Schlesinger's index classified no state as having a very weak governor and identified eight as having very strong governors (Beyle, 1983, 1988). For the most part, governors are now considered to have both the formal and informal tools to provide executive leadership of state administration (Bernick, 1979).

Notwithstanding formal power enhancements, some contemporary scholars suggest that being a governor in the 1980s may be more difficult than previously. Larry Sabato (1983) contends that in many states there is still a fragmented administrative establishment. National devolution of programs has given governors more responsibilities to their respective states and local governments. At a time when governors need to provide more executive leadership and policy guidance they may be neglecting these roles. Muchmore (Beyle and Muchmore, 1983:82) has noted the "custodial relationship" or limited gubernatorial involvement of most governors with the agencies of the executive branch, despite the governors' "strong position to direct, control, plan, organize, evaluate, and coordinate" their activities. In the same vein, Abney and Lauth argue that governors are not the chief administrators of state government that they could and should be. This is "not because they lack formal powers, but because they are apparently personally incapable or disinclined to use those powers which they possess" (1983:48).

Budget authority, reorganization powers, appointment powers, and tenure potential give governors some means of influencing and controlling the bureaucracy, particularly top-level administrators (Wright, 1967). Several studies suggest, however, that despite a governor's arsenal of formal weapons, administrative policy making often occurs in the absence of appropriate gubernatorial guidance. One explanation of this phenomenon is that informal tools and situational resources may be as important as formal tools in executive empowerment (Weinberg, 1977; Bernick, 1979; Sigelman and Smith, 1981). Nelson C. Dometrius (1979) has reported on the limited efficacy of formal gubernatorial powers. In a similar vein, Weinberg (1977) has noted the importance of gubernatorial interest and crisis management in leadership of state administration. The situational and personal resources governors possess can make a considerable difference in gubernatorial power, but because these resources vary tremendously among the fifty states, case studies highlighting over time one governor's style do not allow a systematic analysis of this form of gubernatorial influence.

Quality of the Occupants

Not only has the office of governor been transformed but a similar turn-around has occurred in the character of the occupants of that office. The shift from a "personalized" to an "institutionalized" governorship has resulted from a confluence of forces—structural and other reforms, changes in federal-state relations, and a higher quality of persons serving as governors (Beyle and Muchmore, 1983). Sabato notes that "if governors were measured against one another as individuals and on accomplishments, those elected to office after 1963 would have a decided edge" (1983:54). Being governor is now a high-prestige job from which many legal-structural constraints of the past have been significantly reduced. A higher-caliber person is attracted to and holds this office in an intergovernmental environment that emphasizes the state as a unit of governance.

State Legislatures

Revitalization of the "Sometime Governments"

Governors who attempt to exercise executive leadership must contend with the powerful and competing forces manifested in state legislative bodies. Although the office of the governor (and its occupants) has increased in influence, there is an unstated premise in much of the literature that executive influence has increased in relation to both the state administrative bureaucracy and the state legislature. The influence of the second "overhead" institutional actor, the legislature, has not remained constant, however. On the contrary, major and far-reaching changes have occurred in state legislative capabilities and functioning.

During the first half of this century, state legislatures were characterized by malapportionment, inflexible rules regarding structure and procedures, amateurism, inadequate facilities and staff, high turnover, and poor-quality officeholders (Citizens Conference, 1971). Legislative reforms of the 1960s and 1970s have transformed these so-called sometime governments into a more formidable and also a more equal actor in the public policy process.

Structural and Procedural Capacities

In the last three decades state legislatures have become more representative, functional, and accountable. The Citizens Conference on State Legislatures (CCSL) offered in 1971 a classification scheme by which to evaluate legislative performance in the states. The CCSL scheme grouped criteria and recommendations under five categories called FAIIR (functionality, accountability, information-handling capacity, independence, and representativeness). Each of these concepts was given an operational meaning and translated into a measurable, quantitative score. For each of the fifty state legislatures an aggregate numerical score was derived. The results were not flattering, to say the least. The subsequent response, however, was rather astounding.

According to a report of the U.S. Advisory Commission on Intergovernmental Relations (1985), state legislatures have "changed significantly" on thirty-eight of the seventy-three CCSL recommendations. Adopted reforms consistent with FAIIR recommendations include many changes: the switch to annual sessions (functionality), creation and increase in the number of single-member districts (accountability), increased professional staff (information-handling capacity), establishment of legislative evaluation units (independence), and higher compensation levels (representativeness).

Like the governorship, state legislatures were ill-equipped to govern effectively in the first half of the twentieth century, in part because constitutions were outdated. The modernization of state constitutions which occurred in the 1960s and 1970s had two impacts on legislative functioning. One was the lifting of structural and procedural restrictions such as those pertaining to session length, chamber and committee size, and compensation (ACIR, 1985). A common constitutional constraint abolished by states was the mandating of short biennial sessions. Annual sessions give state legislatures more time to carry out duties that have grown astronomically in the latter half of this century because of increased government scope, size, and services and increasingly complex intergovernmental relationships. The number of states holding annual sessions increased from ten in 1955, to twenty-six in 1969, to thirty-seven in 1981.

Second, there has been a shift from constitutionally mandated legislative procedures and structural requirements to statutory law as a basis for legislative operations. States have streamlined their committee systems and offered higher salaries. Between 1955 and 1981, the average number of committees in state houses and senates decreased, respectively, from thirty to twenty and from twenty-four to fifteen. Most states now provide compensation packages that include salary, retirement, and insurance benefits, features that, arguably, might attract a higher caliber of legislator. Only nine states continue to restrict legislative salaries through constitutional constraints. These modernized constitutions provide both the flexibility and the capacity that legislatures need to govern in times of rapid change.

Other improvements in legislative capacities consistent with FAIIR principles include increased office space and facilities as well as more and better staff assistance. By 1982 eighteen states provided private offices for house members and twenty-six states did likewise for senate members. Most states have legislative councils and libraries to provide research, fiscal, and bill-drafting assistance. In addition, the number and type of legislative staff have increased. Along with clerical support, which is the norm, many states provide administrative and professional staff for both individual legislators and legislative committees. In 1982 forty-one states reported that most of their committees had professional support. Legislative leaders in thirty-two states had professional staff.

Legislative Oversight of Administration

What impact have the changes in legislative capacities and capabilities had on state administration? Partially because of its improved capacity, state legislatures have embraced additional and innovative techniques of legislative oversight of state administration. State legislatures have attempted to restore a perceived imbalance between legislative and bureaucratic power. Most techniques of bureaucratic control adopted over the last two decades involve a broader role for legislatures in overseeing public policy execution. They are characteristic of attempts to exercise direct, active, and centralized surveillance types of legislative oversight, often referred to as "police-patrol" strategies. These techniques contrast with the more customary "fire-alarm," indirect, episodic, and decentralized legislative surveillance (McCubbins and Schwartz, 1984; Miller, 1987).

Some of the most common oversight techniques adopted in recent years are auditing, evaluation units, administrative rule review, sunset laws, and appropriation of federal funds. By 1970 half of the states had audit or evaluation units. Administrative rule review has become one of the most prevalent oversight techniques, with thirty-eight states establishing administrative rule review committees. In 1982 thirty-six states had sunset laws. Finally, after years of conflict between executives and legislatures over the issue, most state legislatures are able to review and/or appropriate federal funds. According to the ACIR (1985), nineteen states have a "strong ability" to exercise control over federal funds and only eight states have a "limited ability" to do so.

Administrators' Perceptions of Institutional Control and Influence

We have cited and highlighted the significant growth in the size and scope of the administrative establishment(s) in state government(s). We have also reviewed the changing roles and strengths of governors and legislatures in recent decades. We now focus on the administrative leaders (agency heads) of this enlarged administrative component. More specifically, we probe their views on the control, oversight, review, and influence asserted over them by the governor and the legislature. For this purpose we rely on data collected from the ASAP surveys conducted in the 1960s, 1970s, and 1980s.

Table 7.5 reports the responses of state agency heads to a set of four questions included in the five ASAP surveys. The questions presented the top-level administrators with choices concerning their perceptions of institutional relationships with the governor and legislature. Two queries elicited responses on the issue of control and oversight influence—one on control actually exercised and one on preferred control. Another item assessed budgetary bias in governor-legislator behavior while a fourth question probed support for agency goals. Taken together, the four items deal with aspects of administrative agency purposes (goals), processes (budget), and power relationships.

We approach the responses tabulated in Table 7.5 with an institutionally based hypothesis. The rise of the governor from figurehead to executive leader should be reflected in the perceptions of top-level state administrators. We would expect that the enhanced position of governors across the fifty states would lead agency heads to acknowledge the increased control, influence, and support of governors rather than legislators.

A scan of the row percentages for the governor category in each of the four items shows that over time the "stronger-governor" hypothesis is not clearly supported by the data. For one or two items a modest rise in the gubernatorial percentages from 1964 to 1974 hint at an executive-oriented trend. Since 1974, however, the proportions for the gubernatorial alternatives have remained stable or have even declined slightly.

How might this stability in administrators' perceptions over two decades be explained? Several possibilities occur to us. These include explanations ranging from substantive interpretations to methodological matters.

Methodological Issues

An important methodological issue in social science research is the question of validity. Do the questions, data, and results measure what the researcher intends to measure? In this instance, do the four queries posed to agency heads accurately measure the influence and institutional status of the governor in relation to state administration? We believe that the items have face or content validity that can withstand careful scrutiny.

A second methodological issue involves the sample of administrators responding to the surveys. Several more specific and subsidiary problems arise here, which need not be discussed in detail. Two significant problems with the sample are that there was a larger universe of agency heads for the 1974, 1978, and 1984 surveys than in 1964 and 1968 and there may be bias in response rates.

Only thirty to thirty-five agency heads in each state were included in the two surveys in the 1960s. The number of agencies included in the last three surveys was in the range of sixty to seventy per state. One strategy to deal with this problem is to analyze the responses of agency heads only from comparable agencies across the five surveys. That analysis produced results consistent with those shown in Table 7.5, that is, no strong or consistent pro-gubernatorial trends in the responses.

The problem of response rate bias is less easily accommodated. It is possible to say that the characteristics of those responding to the ASAP surveys showed no important departures or differences from figures produced by alternate external data sources. Two alternate indicators were gender proportions and turnover rates. Otherwise, we can only note that there were no apparent and exceptionally high (or low) response rates by type of agency or region of country.

Substantive Interpretations: Comparative Influence

Let us now turn to possible substantive explanations for the consistency and stability of responses concerning gubernatorial guidance and oversight of state administrators. A first and possibly radical explanation is that institutional change (or "reform") makes little if any difference in the ability of governors to influence state administration. This interpretation is termed radical because it runs counter to the conventional wisdom that reorganization and related structural reform produce positive results in the governor's ability to direct state administration. Two (or more) decades of enhancing the position and personage(s) of those occupying the governor's office should enable them to leave a deeper and stronger imprint on the perceptions and preferences of top administrative officials. In its extreme form this avenue of explanation challenges the oft-quoted phrase of Alexander Pope: "Forms of government fools contest; what 'ere is best administered is best." Present data and analysis techniques do not permit us to

Table 7.5. Institutional Orientations of American State Administrators: Perspectives on Power, Process, and Purposes (in percent[a])

	1964 (N = 933)	1968 (N = 991)	1974 (N = 1,587)	1978 (N = 1,393)	1984 (N = 1,121)
Who exercises greater control over your agency's affairs?					
Governor	32	37	46	41	41
Each about the same	22	25	26	22	22
Legislature	44	36	26	36	34
Other and not available	2	2	3	1	2
	100	100	101	100	99
What type of control do you prefer?					
Governor	42	46	50	49	51
Independent commission	28	[b]	30	29	27
Legislature	24	21	14	19	16
Other and not available	5	33	6	3	6
	99	100	100	100	100

Who has the greater tendency
to reduce budget requests?

Governor	25	29	30	36	35
Each about the same	b	b	b	30	19
Legislature	60	55	41	33	42
Other and not available	15	16	29	1	4
	100	100	100	100	100

Who is more sympathetic to
the goals of your agency?

Governor	55	54	58	53	59
Each about the same	14	15	9	9	8
Legislature	20	19	25	33	28
Other and not available	11	12	8	5	5
	100	100	100	100	100

Source: Wright, 1990.
[a]Percentages may not add to 100 because of rounding.
[b]Denotes that this alternative was not posed for the survey year.

rule out this interpretation, but we think it is among the less likely sources of the stable status of the governor in relation to state administration (Meier, 1980).

A second reason for stable gubernatorial status in the eyes of state agency heads might arise from gubernatorial selectivity and priority setting. Perhaps the easiest way to indicate this interpretation is to note that not all state agencies and their nested programs and policies are equal, especially in the eyes of the governor. One common theme in the advice given new governors is to set their aims on achieving only a few important policy goals (National Governors' Association, 1978). The behavioral consequence of this prescription is that governors tend to devote attention to only a few policies, programs, or issues in highly selective administrative arenas (Weinberg, 1977). As noted previously, the need for crisis management and differing situational and personal resources may lead to selectivity in the exercise of gubernatorial oversight.

Gubernatorial control, budgetary review, and goal support may be consciously intended to make a significant impact on only two, three, or four agencies during a governor's term (Hebert, Brudney, and Wright, 1983). This small number of intended effects may be reduced or totally submerged in responses from twenty, twenty-five, or thirty agency heads in each state. If we had an indicator of how many and which agencies were singled out for special gubernatorial attention in each state from the 1960s through the 1980s, we could explore this explanation empirically.

There is a third substantive basis for expecting comparatively constant gubernatorial positioning in relation to state administration. The clue to this line of analysis emerges from the word *comparatively*. Each of the four items arrayed in Table 7.5 contains institutional alternatives other than the governor, with the primary one, of course, being the legislature. Posed in this manner, the questions required a forced and comparative choice by the administrators. Stated differently, the respondents were confronted with a mandated zero-sum trade-off between the governor and the legislature. The real world of administrative control, review, and support, however, may not conform to the institutional premise(s) built into the question items displayed in Table 7.5.

Two possible sets of occurrences may be considered. In both instances, basic institutional influence relationships might have changed in important ways. The views of top agency personnel, however, might not reflect these shifts because of the aggregate and comparative conditions represented in Table 7.5.

First, imagine the following simplified and hypothetical condition. Suppose that in half the states gubernatorial status increased among top administrators while in the other half of the states legislative strength was on the rise. These contrasting shifts in institutional status could be offsetting across the states, canceling out changes in other states and producing essentially stable patterns over the years. A variant of this offsetting pattern would be for half the agency heads in each state to acknowledge a shift toward gubernatorial primacy in these four arenas of comparative choice while the other half report a rise in legislative primacy. The proportion (one-half) chosen for these illustrations is obviously arbitrary and unlikely, whether for states or agency heads. This simplicity, however, helps highlight the complexity, diversity, variety, incremental, and even contradictory character of shifting patterns of institutional orientations across the far-flung state administrative establishment.

Second, consider a line of reasoning about comparative executive-legislative influence that directly challenges the nature of zero-sum relationships posited between governors and legislatures. The point has often been made that presidential-congressional power relations are not like a Pennsylvania Avenue teeter-totter with seats at the White House and Capitol Hill. Especially when it involves national administrative agencies, there is no fundamental political law which says that as congressional influence rises, executive influence naturally declines (by an equal or greater amount). This non-zero-sum (positive-sum) influence pattern has seldom been applied to the state level and even more rarely explored with respect to state administrative agencies.

We propose that the positive-sum influence pattern is relevant to state government and state administration. We suggest that it is present in respondents' perceptions reported in Table 7.5. Moreover, we think it makes a major contribution to explaining why the gubernatorial proportions are fairly constant across the three decades tapped by the ASAP surveys.

The positive-sum pattern can be explained in straightforward institutional terms. Governors have become more capable, energetic, and influential over the past three decades for the reasons mentioned earlier in this chapter. But legislatures have also become more capable, energetic, and influential over the same time span. These changes have not been merely offsetting. Rather, both governors and legislatures are in the position of exerting greater guidance, direction, and influence over state administrative agencies. In comparative terms, however, administrators perceive and report that the relative institutional positions of the two political entities are roughly the same in the 1980s as they were in the 1960s.

Starting in the 1970s, the ASAP surveys allowed for and sought to measure positive-sum influence patterns. This was accomplished by adding questions that are best described as self-standing or independent indicators of influence. Neither the specifics nor the details of this line of analysis can be explored here. Instead, we report only a few summary percentages and consider the broader implications arising from this approach.

Independent (Self-Standing) Indicators of Influence

State agency heads were asked in the 1978 and 1984 ASAP surveys to indicate independently the level of gubernatorial and legislative influence (from high to low or none) exerted over four agency activities. The four arenas in which influence levels were calibrated were major policy changes, total budget level, budgets for specific programs, and agency rules and regulations. The separate responses for governors and legislators are indicated in Table 7.6. (Only the percentages of administrators reporting high influence are shown.)

There are several ways in which these data could be discussed and contrasted; there are also multiple methods by which explanatory analyses could be conducted. For present purposes only two discussion strategies will be pursued: comparisons between 1978 and 1984 results for the gover-

Table 7.6. High Level of Gubernatorial and Legislative Influence over Agency Activities (in percent)

Areas of Activity	Governor	Legislature
Major Policy Changes		
1978	57	47
1984	57	47
Total Budget Level		
1978	70	67
1984	74	66
Specific Program Budgets		
1978	63	67
1984	60	63
Agency Rules/Regulations		
1978	34	32
1984	28	23

Source: Wright, 1990.
Note: N = 1,393 in 1978; N = 1,121 in 1984.

nor and legislature separately and comparison of the percentages of the governor with those of the legislature. (We minimize any discussion of comparisons among the decision areas.)

The marginal percentages indicating a high level of influence by the governor remain remarkably constant between 1978 and 1984 for all four decision areas. Similarly, the proportions are strikingly similar for legislative influence when 1978 and 1984 percentages are compared for three of the four decision areas. Only for decisions on agency rules is there a notable difference (nine percentage points) between 1978 and 1984 figures. These independent measures of influence levels help confirm the perceived stability of both gubernatorial and legislative oversight of state administration.

Comparisons of the percentages across the executive-legislative institutional gulf lead to additional observations. With the exception of decisions on budgets for specific programs, the proportions rating gubernatorial influences as high regularly exceed the percentages for legislatures, but the differences are modest or small between the two institutions.

Also noteworthy is the overall magnitude of the percentages. For example, two-thirds or more of the agency heads in both 1978 and 1984 indicated that both the governor and the legislature asserted a high degree of influence on the agency's total budget levels. These and the other percentage levels underscore the point that the exercise of influence over administrative actions is not necessarily a zero-sum game between governors and legislatures.

More conceptual thinking as well as empirical analysis remains to be done before we can paint a complete picture of the various shadings and patterns that show executive-legislative dynamics in relation to state administration. The availability of data over time might enable us to shift the picture from a series of snapshots to a moving picture. In either case, the significance of state government and state administration in contemporary public affairs should elevate conceptual and empirical analyses of this topic from the status of a newsreel short to a full-length feature film.

Concluding Observations

The imperative need for bureaucratic accountability is a constant theme in the literature on executive leadership of administration in the American political system. That imperative is closely matched with the perceived difficulty of attaining an adequate degree of accountability among top-level administrators. Coleman Ransone both focused and expanded on a discussion of these themes at the state level more than three decades ago. We have attempted to deepen and sharpen the furrows in the field he plowed.

We assess trends in the perceived accountability relationships of state agency heads to the state's chief executive—the governor. The data on administrators' perceptions span twenty years, across three decades from 1964 through 1984. During this period the office of governor (and its occupants) experienced a dramatic rise in power, prestige, and prerogatives. That institutional change led us to hypothesize that this alteration would result in rising levels of perceived control, constraint, and influence by the governor over state administration.

This singular and elementary supposition was not confirmed by results. There was a modest and consistent rise in the perceived influence of the governor over state administration from 1964 to 1974. Since the latter date, however, the governor's perceived influence has either stabilized or declined slightly. When four different indicators of influence are considered, the evidence appears convincing. Despite dramatic changes in the institutional strength of the governorship, the perceived influence of that office over state administration (as reported by agency heads) has not changed appreciably. Executive government has not produced heightened oversight by the governor or the expected rise in administrative accountability.

Do the results of the successive ASAP surveys of state administrators indicate that state agencies are any less accountable to governors now than in the past? Or do the findings suggest that there has been no increase in the accountability of state administrators? We think that negative replies hold for both of these queries. We contend that a careful appraisal of the survey results permits inferences that reinforce, rather than deny, the nature of institutional controls over state administration. The inferences about continuing and potentially potent checks on state administration rest on two interpretations.

First, questions about executive oversight and control of administration have, historically, tended to be viewed in institutional isolation. That is, administrators are questioned and administration is assessed on the basis of an exclusive executive orientation, in this case, toward the governor. This splendid isolation, however, does not easily or closely approximate the real world of state administration. Perhaps the most evident and important modification is introduced by the presence of state legislatures.

Thus when questions about power, purpose(s), and processes are put to administrators in comparative terms—that is, executive versus legislative influence(s)—it is not surprising that governors fail to show increasing dominance of state administration. Governors may attain a plurality or an occasional majority recognition of primacy in administrative oversight. That primacy, however, is not on the ascendancy in terms that are relative to legislative oversight of state administration.

Framing the issue of institutional oversight and administrative accountability in executive-legislative (comparative) terms leads to a second interpretation. Rather than a zero-sum influence pattern involving executive-legislative influence(s) over the bureaucracy, we suggest the existence of a positive-sum influence pattern. That is, both the executive and the legislative branches of state government have found the means to enhance or otherwise increase their own independent influence over state administration.

Regardless of increases over time in the perceived influence of the governor, legislature, or both, we can document simultaneously high levels of influence for both the governor and the legislature. Substantially more than a majority of responding administrators acknowledge that both the governor and the legislature exercise high influence over total budget levels and budgets for specific programs. Approximately half of the agency heads report that both the governor and legislature exert a high level of influence on major policy changes involving their respective agencies.

Administrators' recognition of a high level of influence for both the governor and legislature suggests that simultaneous accountability to both institutions may be a realistic view of the accountability claims that administrative agencies confront. In a study exploring gubernatorial leadership of state administration in a changing political context, it is not an inconsequential finding that state agency heads consistently attribute a significant level of influence to the governor. Nor is it inconsequential that state legislatures are also evident and active participants in administrative oversight.

Although our findings encapsule a predominantly stable twenty-year pattern of perceived gubernatorial influence and oversight of state administration, we note that there may be wide variations in this pattern. We have painted with a broad brush across the canvas this research represents. A continuation of our analysis entails investigating the correlates that may affect the institutional orientations of ASAP administrators.

There is, for instance, considerable diversity among the people who constitute state agency heads. There is also substantial variation in the degree of formal powers at the governor's disposal. These are two correlates which analysis has revealed as potentially important explanatory variables—the method of appointment of the administrator and the extent of formal powers of the governor (Wright, 1967). State agency heads come to their jobs by several means. The methods range from career or merit (civil service) selection (about one-fourth of the administrators in the five survey years) to gubernatorial appointment (around 40 percent with or without legislative consent). Only a small proportion (around 5 percent) are selected by popular election.

We might hypothesize that the degree of gubernatorial involvement in the appointment of an administrator is positively related to gubernatorial influence and control. Similarly, we might expect governors with extensive formal powers to exert more influence than governors with institutionally weak power bases. Future analysis should enlarge and refine the initial and partial sketch provided here. That analysis could provide fine-line details on aspects of the extensive art form that constitutes administrative accountability in state government.

Acknowledgment

The authors wish to express their thanks to the Earhart Foundation of Ann Arbor, Michigan, for support and assistance in gathering the survey data in the 1970s and 1980s.

8 THE CHANGED POLICY CONTEXT OF THE STATES; OR, WHY GREAT INDIVIDUALS OUGHT NOW TO BE ELECTED GOVERNOR

Donald T. Wells

"Although much less sought after than 'in the days of the Fathers,' when a State governor sometimes refused to yield precedence to the President of the United States, the governorship is still . . . a post of some dignity, and affords an opportunity for the display of character and talents" (Bryce, 1910:500).

The quotation from James Bryce is a classic example of "damning with faint praise." The point made is well taken, however: something important happened to the governorship in the evolution of the American political system. To use Lord Bryce's quaint phrase, in "the days of the Fathers," the states generally were viewed as sovereignties (Graves, 1964:60).

This mode of thinking meant that for much of early American history, public policy was state-centered. And since states characteristically maintained an attitude bordering on isolation from each other and the central government, such thinking meant that most day-to-day public policy was specific state-centered. In such an environment some state governors did refuse "to yield precedence to the President of the United States."

Yet the quotation from Bryce is misleading to the extent that it implies that governors in the formative period possessed strong powers and were vigorous in the exercise of those powers. To the contrary, the fear of tyranny resulted in a substantial weakening of the governorship (compared to the colonial governors) in the first state constitutions. Leslie Lipson reports the comment of a delegate to the North Carolina constitutional convention to the effect that the state's constitution gave the governor just enough power "to sign the receipt for his salary" (1939:14). And as astute an observer of early American politics as James Madison referred to the governors of the newly independent states as "little more than cyphers" (quoted in Sabato, 1983:4). This weakening, along with several other factors, meant that the office generally among the states did not appeal to the best potential leaders, even though the post did retain "some dignity." As a result, a modern British observer of American politics, Harold Laski, reported a bimodal distribution of American governors: either "second rate politicians" in the one group or in the other persons interested in a national political career vis-à-vis the state governorship as a "stage in the ascent" (Laski, 1949:146). Among American observers states generally and governors specifically came under harsh criticism from a number of quarters in the 1940s and 1950s (see especially Allen, 1949; Sanford, 1967). Ironically, the harshest criticism seemed to come when the indicators of change were increasingly apparent.

The "modernization of the governorship" has been well documented elsewhere (see especially, Lipson, 1939; Ransone, 1956; Kallenbach, 1966; Sabato, 1983). Leslie Lipson, in almost prophetic fashion, subtitled his book *From Figurehead to Leader*. Sabato hailed "Goodbye to Good-Time Charlie," the premodern governor, and analyzed the factors producing the transformation of the office of governor during the years 1950 to 1975. He described the process most succinctly: "The transformation of the American governor—from near omnipotent colonial to emasculated 'cypher' to the modern new breed—is now apparent" (1983:198). Although governors have not been elevated to the level of "omnipotence" of the colonial governors, they are now in a position to make a significant difference in the political, economic, and social life of their states. As Sabato observed, "The resultant new breed of governor . . . will continue to have enormous significance for government at all levels in the United States" (1983:201).

This chapter is an effort to elucidate one area in which governors can make the most important difference—the area of public policy. Recent general literature on the office of the governor recognizes the importance of gubernatorial behavior for public policy in the states. The opening sentence of what is perhaps still the definitive study of the office emphasizes this fact: "During the last fifty years the American governor has emerged as a policy leader of no mean proportions" (Ransone, 1956:3). In such previous works, the primary emphasis was either on the role of the governor in policy formation (the politics of the office) or on the management role of the governor relative to state program departments. Given that the gubernatorial reform movement was largely management-based, it is not surprising that most of the literature concentrated on the governor as manager of the state administrative apparatus. Thus considerable attention was given to such matters as structural reform (i.e., the integration of a disintegrated executive branch), to the centralization of decision making (i.e., planning and staffing in the executive branch to accomplish a coherent gubernatorial program), and to budgeting and personnel reforms. In the general literature, then, structural reform and organizational design were the keys to the governor's effective performance as policy leader.

In this chapter I propose to expand this view of the policy role of the governor through an analysis of the changed policy environment within the American states. The method used is an expansion of what Charles Perrow (1977), in a study of program implementation, referred to as the revelatory strategy. At base, the revelatory strategy is reasoned thought about a program's history. Using this research strategy, I ask whether an examination of the policy environment suggests important general propositions relative to gubernatorial leadership in public policy. Admittedly, this approach means that the chapter is somewhat reflective. But as Coleman Ransone, Jr., once observed in a conversation with me, "Why we are into so much research and so little reflection on the meaning of what we have discovered is a mystery to me." Additionally, I emphasize that there is a substantial factual program history base in a number of policy areas for the observations and conclusions drawn here. The public policy literature includes a large number of case studies in a variety of policy areas. In this chapter, then, I attempt from an analysis of the state policy environment to draw out generalizable principles, motifs, and lessons for gubernatorial leadership and public policy.

The following three propositions are addressed:

Proposition 1: As with the formative period, public policy in the United States is remarkably state-centered.

Proposition 2: The policy environment within the states has changed dramatically in the last quarter of the twentieth century.

Proposition 3: The combined effect of propositions 1 and 2 is to give the "new breed of governors" unique opportunity for policy leadership.

The first proposition may be referred to as the opportunity dimension, the second as the contextual dimension, and the third as the leadership dimension. The discussion that follows is based on these propositions.

Proposition 1: The Opportunity Dimension— State-Centered Public Policy

In academic circles about twenty years ago it became something of an article of faith that public policies in the United States were inherently intergovernmental. This meant that the policy process in any given area was spread over all levels in such a way that no particular level retained control or dominant influence over the content and implementation of policy. As a result, most policy analysts downplayed the proposition that responsibility for policy is located a little differently at different levels. To them, policy was all mixed in everywhere so that little could be said about the policy process at any given level.

One of the important lessons to be drawn from case studies is that public policy is still largely state-centered. It is true that policy is not the exclusive domain of any single level and that it does involve the broad sharing of responsibility among all levels. But the important word in that statement is *exclusive*. Although states do not have exclusive responsibility in any policy area, general policy control is located more or less in the states (of course, states reflect different policy initiatives in various policy areas).

Although case studies illustrating this fact are numerous (see Henig, 1985), state-centered public policy is most clearly seen in a subset of environmental policy known as hazardous waste policy. Hazardous wastes may be divided for policy purposes into three groups—solid waste, toxic chemical waste, and nuclear waste (itself divided into two subgroups—low-level and high-level). Responsibility for solid waste policy, historically, has been solidly with the states. The states' exclusive responsibility is diluted only in that the national government monitors state and local facilities. Toxic chemical waste policy is an excellent example of the regulatory device known as partial preemption. In this strategy, national legislation, the Resource Conservation and Recovery Act, vests states with primary responsibility with the exception that if the states do not act, the national government will. As a result, states have acted and have assumed primary responsibility for toxic chemical waste policy. The Low Level Nuclear Waste Act is more direct in providing for state responsibility—almost to the point of a direct-order form of national regulation of the states. The act mandates that the states shall provide capacity for storage of low-level nuclear waste and specifies that action shall be on the basis of regional compacts. High-level nuclear waste—spent fuel rods from electric power plants, residuals from defense production, and the like—remains the responsibility of the national government. An examination of this policy set shows that responsibility is more or less located primarily at the state level.

Thus if the situation in this policy subset is generalizable, and I believe it is, policy in the United States, as in the formative period, is largely state-centered. A larger study of federalism expressed the situation as follows: "Granted, responsibility for policy shifts over time, and it is 'like skating on thin ice' to picture policy control as being 'sealed off' between levels. A common sense description of who mostly does what at which level is a far more accurate view than the misleading (if not silly) assertion that policy is fully shared in such a way that no level performs any distinctive function or that policy responsibility is totally sealed off by level in the federal system. A common sense description should emphasize who *primarily* does what at which level and with what effects" (Hamilton and Wells, 1990:107–8). When public policy is so viewed, what is most striking is the dominant responsibility of the states.

Additionally, there has been a pervasive revitalization of state activity in the area of public policy—a process frequently referred to as policy momentum at the state level. To put the matter simply, when one examines American public policy the most striking fact that emerges is that although "policy paralysis" exists in many areas at the national level (Lowi, 1969) there is substantial activity at the state level. For several reasons, national policy momentum has been lost, in part the victim of what Theodore J. Lowi called hyperpluralism. National institutions have become timid in the face of hostile groups, including some of the nation's most influential political leaders. A further complicating factor is that national decision makers must seek a general policy for a very generalized and diffused problem. As a result, they often resolve their problem by taking largely symbolic action, as was the case with the Resource Conservation and Recovery Act (Conlan and Abrams, 1981:19). But paralysis in Washington does not necessarily mean paralysis in state capitals.

The occurrence of national policy paralysis and state policy momentum raises a number of interesting questions. (Obviously, viewed from a perspective of federalism, the situation could be seen as healthy.) One of the most likely outcomes of the situation is substantial conflict between the states and the nation. This possibility is already present in the hazardous waste area. A good example has to do with the transportation of nuclear waste. Existing regulations by the Nuclear Regulatory Commission and the Department of Transportation, being as kind as possible, have to be described as loose, a commonly held view among analysts (e.g., Choi, 1984:18). Policy paralysis at the national level has meant that national agencies have done little to tighten up those loose regulations. States, however, may adopt standards that are inconsistent with—more stringent than—national standards (see *Huron Portland Cement Co. v. City of Detroit*, 362 U.S. 440 [1960]). Additionally, recent decisions of the Supreme Court seem to suggest that a state may shut down a nuclear waste storage and disposal operation if the state determines that the plant and its operation are uneconomical or unreliable (Choi, 1984:14). Both the states of Washington (the Radioactive Waste Storage and Transportation Act of 1980) and South Carolina (the South Carolina Radioactive Waste Transportation and Disposal Act of 1980) have taken steps to put "teeth" into policy. (The Washington act was declared unconstitutional by the U.S. District Court.) Whatever the immediate results of such state action, the situation raises some highly significant "what if" questions. What if a state governor stops nationally operated trucks carrying radioactive wastes and prohibits their entrance into the state? What if a governor shuts down a nationally licensed or operated (as Hanford, Washington, or Barnwell, South Carolina) radioactive waste facility? What if a state governor, to paraphrase Andrew Jackson, said, "The Feds have made their decision, now let them carry it out in my state"?

This is not to predict that the United States will experience a president-governor "shoot-out at high noon" every other day. Obviously, conflicts in all policy areas will continue to be resolved by and large through negotiation and bargaining as they have been in the past. But the potential does bring the federal system back to "the days of the Fathers." The United States may very well be once again in a situation in which state governors occasionally refuse "to yield precedence to the President of the United States."

A second outcome of state policy momentum may be the localization or regionalization of national policy concerns. In the regulatory federalism area, much has been written lately about the "nationalization of the states," a concept that refers to the use of national regulatory power to assure uniformity and commonality among the states in implementing national policy objectives (Hanus, 1981; Wells, 1987). Two observers who monitored this aspect of national-state relations concluded that "it is a mechanism which challenges the very essence of federalism as a noncentralized system of separate legal jurisdictions and instead relies upon a unitary vision involving hierarchically related central and peripheral units" (Dubnick and Gitelson, 1981:56). If this is the case, the concept is a basic challenge to the assertion that policy is state-centered. State discretion would be virtually eliminated in favor of national prescription of policy.

In fact, the opposite of "nationalization of the states" may be happening. This policy situation has been referred to as the "localization or regionalization of national policy goals" (see Hamilton and Wells, 1990, for a fuller discussion). This concept refers to the displacement of national policy objectives with state and/or local objectives. This displacement occurs in several policy areas but seems strongest in housing, education, and the environment. For example, in a perceptive study of the Housing and Community Development Act, Margaret Wrightson (1986) attempted to identify what policy goals were being implemented. The intent of the act was clearly to provide low-income families housing opportunities in areas where housing had previously been unavailable to them—a policy known as the spatial deconcentration of low-income housing. Instead, local decision makers modified the intent of the policy so as to provide low-income housing in areas that "needed it." As a result, low-income families remained frozen in areas with inadequate schools and other services. In essence, the intent of spatial deconcentration was transformed into a policy of spatial concentration. In Wrightson's words, this local displacement of national policy goals raised "the potentially damaging issue of *what policy is being implemented*" (1986:272). And in education, substantial media attention has been directed to schools previously integrated that have reverted back to all-white or all-black status (*Atlanta Constitution*, eight-part series starting October 27, 1987, p. 1). Most of the data indicate that those districts that resegregated did so as a matter of deliberate local decision.

The important point is that public policies in the United States are by and large state-centered. And the policy momentum found at the state and local levels joined with the policy paralysis characteristic of the national government has resulted in the localization and regionalization of national policy objectives. Indeed, the diversity among the states may mean that, as in the formative period, public policy is by and large state-centered. As when Daniel Elazar made the observation, states still are separate "civil communities" (Elazar, 1966).

Proposition 2: The Contextual Dimension—The Changed Nature of State-Centered Public Policy

The second proposition drawn from the public policy environment is that the policy context of the states—and thus the policy issues and opportunities the governor encounters—has changed dramatically in the last quarter of the twentieth century. Again, this proposition is widely recognized in the literature. As early as 1961 an observer of the common interest of governors concluded, "American state governors have gone through a political revolution in the past half-century. Once they were political homebodies with few responsibilities or interests beyond the boundaries of their home states. Today they are immersed in policy-making and partisan politics at the national and even the international level" (Brooks, 1961:vii). More recently, scholars have turned their attention to the question of whether responsibility is being pushed back to the states at a time when problems are becoming more expensive, complex, and intractable (Henig, 1985; Caraley, 1986; Palmer and Sawhill, 1985). It is such work that provokes interest in the dimensions of change in the state policy environment. In what ways are state problems more expensive, complex, and intractable and what are the implications of these developments for state policy environments?

Drawing from the program histories of public policy, the most significant dimensions of change in state policy environments are associated with the words *intergenerational, international,* and *intergovernmental.* And it is because state policies are now infused with intergenerational, international, and intergovernmental dimensions that state policy requires effective leadership on the part of the governor.

Policy and Intergenerational Concern

"For I the Lord thy God am a jealous God, visiting the iniquity of the fathers upon the children to the third and the fourth generation of those who hate me" (Exod. 20:5). Intergenerational sensitivity is not new. As seen in the quote from Exodus, concern for the intergenerational consequences of action is quite old indeed. But again, something important happened to this concern on the way to the twentieth century. When the Ten Commandments were given, the concern was probably for the intergenerational consequences of collective action (the fathers) on the social fabric of the Hebrew people (the children). Later thought modified this view substantially. One line of thought led to the belief in individual accountability for individual actions: "In those days they shall no longer say: 'The fathers have eaten sour grapes and the children's teeth are set on edge.' But every one shall die for his own sin: each man who eats sour grapes, his teeth shall be set on edge" (Jer. 31:29–30). Connected with the extreme individualism of Western civilization and of American society in particular, this view meant that modern Westerners virtually lost sensitivity to intergenerational issues. If Individual X smoked, for example, the health threat was assumed to accrue only to Individual X.

Among the most obvious (bleak?) lessons to be learned from several policy areas is that decisions made and actions taken have significant intergenerational consequences. Thus we now recognize that if Individual X smokes, a health threat accrues not only to Individual X but also to Individuals Y . . . n. The sins of the fathers are directly and personally visited upon the children "unto the third and fourth generation" of those who make mistakes in judgment or who, out of malice, greed, or unconcern, take the wrong actions. Indeed, with the "half-life" associated with most carcinogens, particularly nuclear wastes, the time frame associated with the "third and fourth generation" seems short and seriously in error.

The emerging sensitivity to intergenerational consequences has resulted in a recognition that such a concern is fundamental to most policy areas. We have known for a long time, for example, that one of the most important determinants of whether a given child will attend college is whether that child's parents attended college. And we should have known that the vicious cycle of poverty is simply the intergenerational consequence of the inability of policy at a given time to raise specific families out of poverty. This recognition is spreading even to traditional management areas normally thought to be almost exclusively technical. An extraordinarily interesting editorial in the *Wall Street Journal* relative to the national budget deficit and resultant growing national debt illustrates this point. The editorial pointed to the "need to construct generational accounts that indicate the present value of what each generation is expected to pay, on net, over its lifetime to the government. Such generational accounts would be unaffected by accounting labels and pure changes in the timing of government payments and receipts. They would tell us how different generations will share in the burden of paying for the government's consumption" (Kotlikoff, 1987:6). Laurence Kotlikoff was concerned with the issue of intergenerational redistribution resulting from the deficit. Put simply, is the present generation giving up consumption for future generations by investing in the productive capability of the economy? Or is the present generation living off its grandchildren by personal consumption beyond its willingness to pay? Whatever the answer to such questions, it is apparent that the budget deficit is not simply a question of technical economics. It is an issue of profound intergenerational significance. If our modes of thinking would allow it, we would recognize that most policies have intergenerational significance.

A beginning point in learning how to deal with intergenerational issues may be to describe how decision makers have dealt with them in the past. A schematic that enables us to map governors' responses to intergenerational issues is a start in the development of descriptive theory (see Figure 8.1).

The typology maps the governors' responses on the basis of two variables. The first is sensitivity to intergenerational issues—which is one variable determining the significance the governor attaches to the policy and thus whether it is on the policy agenda. This variable may serve as an indicator of

Figure 8.1. A Typology of Governors' Responses to Intergenerational Issues

Policy Ideology	Intergenerational Sensitive	
	Sensitive	Insensitive
Favorable	P/A	P/I
Unfavorable	O/A	O/I

P = Proponent of Policy	Type 1 = P/A
O = Opponent of Policy	Type 2 = O/A
I = Inactive in Policy Area	Type 3 = P/I
A = Active in Policy Area	Type 4 = O/I

whether a governor will be active or inactive. The other variable is the governor's policy ideology. Here the question is whether the governor is pro-policy or antipolicy (say, pro-/or antienvironment)—an obvious variable in determining whether a governor will be a proponent or opponent of the policy. On the basis of this two-factor schematic, governors can be classified into four different types. Type 1 is the governor who is sensitive to intergenerational effects and favorably oriented toward the policy area. Such a governor will be a policy activist with a long view toward the outcomes of actions and programs. Type 2 governors are sensitive to intergenerational effects but unfavorable toward the policy area. The governor's unfavorable position toward the policy area may be rooted in a variety of causes. These may range from indifference stemming from unfamiliarity with the policy area to hostility arising from ideological preferences. But the governor's sensitivity to intergenerational consequences of action motivates the Type 2 governor toward some action—most often a rhetorical posture in the policy area. Often the Type 2 governor feels considerable ambivalence, perhaps being a "closet" industry advocate but deeply desirous that his or her grandchild be able to swim in the stream behind their country house. As with ambivalents in organizational adaptations, the policy-ambivalent governor tends to be highly creative. Type 3 governors are insensitive to intergenerational effects but favorably oriented toward the policy. These governors tend to view the policy area simplistically and to take a short-run view. Since they are favorably oriented toward the policy area, they will take some action, but the action will tend toward technical solutions designed for the short run. In addition, Type 3 governors will tend to be somewhat dogmatic and impatient with those who are uncomfortable with an uncertain technology. Type 4 governors are insensitive to intergenerational effects and are unfavorably oriented toward the policy ideology. These are the governors who overtly or covertly oppose state response in the policy area.

In addition to the development of descriptive theory for policy with intergenerational consequences, political leadership needs guidance from normative theory as well. Thus the recent emphasis on ethics in public administration is well placed.

The International Scope of State Policy

The second lesson to be learned from significant change in the state policy environment is that state policy now has implications of international dimensions. What is needed in the analysis of public policy is a general application of the concept of "intermestic affairs" used initially in the study of economic policy (Manning, 1977:307). The concept was based on the assumption of an interrelated and integrated international economy. Thus a disruption in economic activity (say, trade flows) would cause disproportionate hardship in particular local areas. This hardship would provoke increased activity in those local areas, providing the basis for more intense political response at the national level. In this way, international economic relations were also interlocal as state-based factors influenced the character of international relations.

Economic policy is the area in which the international activity of the states is most visible, although the environment would certainly rank a close second (see the study of acid rain by Schmandt and Roderick, 1985). As one of the most comprehensive studies of state government activity reported, global economic interdependence's "practical economic impact on American states and localities is now drawing a new range of subnational political actors into the foreign economic policy arena. During the 1970s, the states significantly expanded both their interest and programmatic involvement in international trade and investment activity" (Kline, 1984:81; see also Kline, 1983). One of the major areas of activity is export assistance. All fifty states have agencies specifically vested with export-import responsibilities ranging from technical assistance to direct subsidies. These activities are so significant for exporters that an exporters' guide to state assistance has been published (Posner, 1984). States are also actively involved in efforts to attract foreign investments. John M. Kline reports that such efforts have become a prominent feature of the general economic development activity of states (1984:85). The National Governors' Association reported that governors of forty-seven states led eighty-seven delegations to foreign countries in 1987 (ACIR, 1988:2). Interestingly, this state activity frequently has been in conflict with national policy objectives. At the same time that the national administration was trying to discourage direct foreign investments, a complicating factor was the "newly found aggressiveness with which many American states pursued d.f.i." (Hastedt, 1985:48). The opposite situation also occurs. States engage in restrictive actions, from extensive "Buy American" advertisements to restrictions on foreign purchases of real estate (Kline, 1984:87). In both instances, states displace national policy objectives.

As in intergenerational policy, there is a clear need for the development of a descriptive theory of intermestic affairs. And political leadership needs guidance from normative theory as well. We need more clearly to understand the ethical implications of our actions for all persons in the global community.

State Policy and Intergovernmental Relations

In spite of predictions that the states would be reduced to "field districts of federal departments" (White, 1953:3), the states are alive and well in the federal system. I emphasize again that public policy in the United States is remarkably state-centered and that enough diversity exists among states to justify the conclusion that public policy to a significant degree is specific state-centered. This does not mean, however, that states are islands unto themselves or that they have returned to a posture of isolationism bordering on hostility to other states and the national government. Rather, the states are in a complex set of relationships both vertically with their substate units and the national government and horizontally with other states.

With the extensive literature on intergovernmental relations, it hardly seems necessary to point out that relations with other governments are important features of the state policy context. What needs to be emphasized about the new state intergovernmental assertiveness is that it centers on the policy process, as has been recognized in the general literature (see especially Jones and Thomas, 1976; Henig, 1985).

A new dimension of intergovernmental relations in the policy process that is as yet unrecognized in the general literature has to do with our understanding of decision making, or what is known in policy analysis as policy enactment. Most policy literature treats enactment as if single institutions make enactment decisions in isolation from other branches and levels. As a result, enactments are classified traditionally into legislation, regulations, executive orders, and court decisions. A statute is an enactment made by a legislative body as a discrete action; a regulation is a discrete action of an administrative agency; an executive order is a discrete action of the chief executive of the jurisdiction; and a court decision is a discrete action of a court—albeit all such decisions are made within a context of a field of forces that influences the decision. The problem with this concept is that such discrete enactments seldom if ever happen in the real world.

Most policy enactments are intergovernmental, made in sequence among as well as between levels and branches of government. Enactment is thus a process characterized by bargaining, compromise, and readjustment. Thus when the Congress passes a statute, say, the Resource Conservation and Recovery Act, very little may actually be decided or enacted. The decision of Congress simply sets into motion a process involving many decision makers and political actors at all levels of government. The process is interbranch, involving in a crucial way decisions made by the Environmental Protection Agency and many other agencies, including the courts in an almost immediate sense. The process is also intergovernmental, involving state legislatures, state environmental protection agencies, and state courts, along with a host of local jurisdictions and agencies. What ultimately will be enacted, that is, what chemicals will be controlled in what way and where and how storage of hazardous residuals will occur, is a result of bargaining, compromise, and readjustment among many decision makers over time.

In a larger work, we have suggested that enactments can better be classified into four categories: directive enactments, bargained enactments, influenced (learned) enactments, and process enactments (Hamilton and Wells, 1990). Directive enactments are decisions made by one institution or level in response to an order from an external institution or under threat of a sanction. Cross-cutting requirements and crossover sanctions in federal grants-in-aid are excellent examples of such enactments. State mandates to local governments are another. Bargained enactments are decisions made by one institution or level resulting from negotiation with an external institution. An excellent example of such an enactment is partial preemption, referred to earlier. Specially appointed members of national courts negotiate agreements with local governments on such actions as redistricting, apportionment, and other civil rights cases. They are dramatic "new kids on the block" forms of negotiated enactments. Influenced enactments are decisions made by one institution or level in voluntary response to actions in another institution or level. Model state laws and uniform state legislation are traditional forms of such enactments. The rapid spread of innovation in such areas as child abuse, child seat belt laws, drunk driving legislation, and even educational reform are more recent forms. Process enactments are decisions that are the outcomes of the administrative or programmatic functioning of an institution in interrelationships with other institutions or levels. These involve such things as personal and informal contacts between officials throughout the intergovernmental system (Wright, 1982). They also involve a wide range of agreements between local jurisdictions such as contracts, joint service agreements, and interlocal planning councils.

These four forms of enactment have virtually displaced solo enactments in the policy process. Policy enactments are processes occurring over time and involving interinstitutional and intergovernmental relationships. Unfortunately, only the beginning has been made on studying enactments in the federal system. We need to understand more clearly how the decision process occurs and how it affects what will happen to whom and who will get what as a result of policy enactments. But they demonstrate clearly that the intergovernmental policy context, as with "the old grey mare," simply "ain't what it used to be."

Most specific policy areas reflect a similar degree of change. One of the more important of these areas, and the one most studied, is fiscal federalism. The Advisory Commission on Intergovernmental Relations has documented the changes in fiscal relations between the units of the federal system very well. This documentation exists in a series of annual volumes entitled *Significant Features of Fiscal Federalism*. These volumes contain time-series data that are extremely valuable in understanding fiscal trends between the states and the nation. Two trends are especially important. The first is the decline in national grants to state and local governments. These grants declined by 15 percent between 1980 and 1987—from $105.9 billion in 1980 to $90.2 billion in 1987. The second trend is more important here. In response to reductions in federal aid flow to the states, states have taken constructive responses to modernize and diversify their revenue systems. John Shannon argues that this resiliency of state and local government is the "most significant and most underrated, feature of the American federal system" (1988:17). States took action to diversify their revenue systems. Forty states now have broad-based income taxes and three others have a more restricted income tax. This action, along with an increased reliance on user fees, increased the elasticity of state revenue systems and made the states less dependent on the property tax. States also took action to modernize their tax systems by providing for more equity in those systems. These actions included such features as the exemption of food from sales tax (twenty-six states), the exemption of prescription drugs from sales tax (forty-three states), a circuit-breaker provision for property tax relief for the elderly (thirty-one states), and more progressive income taxes (ACIR, 1985:207). From these developments and the states' activist role in education and welfare reform, Shannon concludes that "state and local officials have demonstrated an outstanding ability to adjust quickly to great changes" (1988:17). Thus he describes federalism as a "world turned upside down" and the "New Federalism" as a system of proactive state policy response. I propose that public policy, as in the formative period, is remarkably state-centered with significant intergovernmental dimensions.

Proposition 3: The Leadership Dimension— The Governor as Policy Leader

The third proposition derived from an examination of public policy is that the "new breed of governors" has a unique opportunity for policy leadership. I have already examined four major parameters of state policy—that public policy in the United States is largely state-centered, that state policies have intergenerational consequences, that state policy has international implications, and that new intergovernmental dimensions to state policy can be identified.

The state-centered nature of public policy in the United States means that governors must be proactive in their posture toward public policy. To be an effective leader, a governor must be committed to making a difference in the way government affects the lives of people in the state (Terry Sanford in Beyle, 1985:x). This does not mean that a governor must be committed to the eternal expansion of policy activity generally or in a specific program area. But it does mean that the governor's most important area of interest must be policy. The governor must be a policy innovator, both in finding new approaches to meeting the needs of people and in modifying old approaches by learning from others. The adage that states do not learn from each other must not be in the policy mind-set of the new breed of governors. The governor must be a policy entrepreneur, selling policy to supportive groups and decision makers in other institutions and at other levels. The governor's legislative program is simply not enough in the new policy context. The governor's marketing strategy may be as important to success as the program. And governors must be policy managers. Governors must be able to see to it that the policy actually works after the enactment decisions are made and implementation has occurred. Thus I emphasize again that the most important area of interest of the new breed of governors must be policy—policy innovation, policy entrepreneurship, and policy management.

What this means is something different from the posture of those governors Sabato referred to as "Good-Time Charlie" governors. The new breed of governor should not be dependent on an external role model for cues on policy issues. The governor should be the role model. The new breed of governor should not capitulate to the superior authority or knowledge of a higher-level decision maker. The governor should be that superior authority. The new breed of governor should not adopt a reactive posture to national policy, interest group activity, or the like. The governor should be the proactive policy leader. And it might be that the republic would be well served if the new breed of governors had the moral courage, if need be, "to refuse to yield precedence to the President of the United States." In this way, certainly much better than through the highly touted but dubious technique of privatization, the nation would reap the advantages of a competitive policy environment.

Most public policies have intergenerational consequences, which have important implications for gubernatorial leadership. One of the more important is that the new breed of governors must be effective risk managers. They must understand the nature of risks, they must be willing to take risks, and they must be open and candid in their relationships with the general public about the risks involved in various actions. Risk theory has long posited the "revealed preference" approach as a guide to decision makers in making choices between competing risk-reduction alternatives (Starr, 1969). Although "what if" is not necessarily a good indicator of the normative value of "what ought to be," the revealed preference approach at least has the value of emphasizing parental responsibilities and rights in decisions affecting children. And it has the practical effect of accomplishing the people's right to know and building public support for the decision made. One author expressed the matter clearly: "There is nothing new about people being exposed to risks, and there is nothing new about their resenting those risks in the absence of compensating benefits. What is new in their response to the risks of modern technologies is their insistence on having a role in deciding how those risks will be managed. . . . The public's increasing assertiveness about risk issues is part of a general growth in the people's feelings of entitlement. . . . And the people become angry when they perceive violations of this evolving social contract" (Fischhoff, 1985:84). This evolving social contract ought to be a general characteristic of state-centered public policy.

Again this means a new breed of governors with behavioral patterns different from those of "Good-Time Charlie" governors. The new breed of governors should not identify with the "statehouse crowd." They should have a sensitivity to the general welfare, in the constitutional sense of that term. The governor should no longer act on the basis of Roger Sherman's recommendation to the Constitutional Convention to the effect that "the people should have as little as possible to do with government." The governor should be the guarantor that the people will make a difference in what the government does and does not do. And governors should not cloak their positions in ambiguity or take refuge behind a "faceless bureaucracy." The governor should be open and candid with the people. In this way, certainly much better than through the highly touted but dubious techniques of the modern accountability movement, the nation would experience the advantages of a responsible policy context.

The international scope of state-centered public policy has important implications for gubernatorial leadership. At base, it means that the new breed of governors must have intermestic sensitivity. Ironically, this may require the return of partisanship to the political posture of the governor. The term *partisan* is often viewed negatively as a reference to a closed-minded ideologue, but I mean it to refer to an individual who is committed to responsible party government and is willing to accept the internal discipline of the party. So understood, partisanship fosters attention to public sentiment and sensitivity to the social, economic, and ideological forces at work in the jurisdiction. It brings a measure of ideological consensus and lasting social values to bear on immediate decisions. Partisanship is both the sensor of intermestic forces at work in the state and one of the criteria by which those forces are evaluated relative to the general public interest.

It may seem strange to advocate a return to partisanship in the context of the international implications of state-centered policy. But again, such a perspective would be a movement away from the political posture of "Good-Time Charlie" governors. It would be a movement away from the traditional provincialism of governors in the direction of a more cosmopolitan stance. The governor should move through the political party to accomplish ideological consensus and policy preference ordering on the complex issues of the day. And certainly, the new breed of governors should reject the "know-nothingism" of the past with its suspicions and ignorance. Relations with other countries are easily amenable to the political exploitation of imaginary foreign threats. The informed governor, exposed to complex issues by prior consideration within the structures of the political party, should be the basis of an informed public. Again, in this way, much better than through the reformist techniques of nonpartisan politics, the nation would reap the benefits of a more general if not cosmopolitan political perspective.

The new intergovernmental dimensions of state-centered policy have important implications for gubernatorial leadership. One of the most important of these implications has to do with the traits of effective policy leadership. Because enactments are processes across institutional and intergovernmental lines, the office of governor now requires individuals who are open and flexible in their thinking. Conversely, the individual who needs closure on decisions will have a difficult time in the current intergovernmental context. Certainly there are occasions that require decisiveness. And in most states, the "buck stops" with the governor. But for a governor to stop the enactment process, ignoring or locking out participants from other institutions and levels, is to court disaster. In a word, the governor must be skilled in bargaining, compromise, and dispute resolution.

This willingness to engage in what is increasingly known as "process politics" (Hummel, 1987) must extend also to the process of bringing issues to the public agenda. It is important to recognize that "underlying every public debate and every formal conflict over policy there is a barely visible process through which issues come to awareness and ideas about them become powerful. . . . These antecedent processes are as crucial to the formation of policy as the processes of discovery in science are crucial to the formation of plausible hypotheses" (Schon, 1971:123). The "Good-Time Charlie" governor may have made peace with or been a willing agent in nondecisions—the process by which issues are prevented from emerging to protect the interests of the few (Bacharach and Baratz, 1970). But the new breed of governor must be active in those antecedent processes that enable the public to formulate and articulate matters of concern for the general welfare. Both in issue definition and policy formation, then, the governor must not insist on closure but be actively involved in stimulating public debate, compromising variant viewpoints, and resolving the inevitable disputes attendant to process politics. In this way, not through the suspect methods of scientific management, the nation can realize the benefits of the highest form of politics—practicing the art of the possible.

All of these implications may seem to suggest that we need an "ideal type" for governor, a superhuman leader impossible to find except in some romanticized political state. Such an implication is not the case. What is involved is quite practical. Lord Bryce speculated on national political leadership in a provocative chapter entitled "Why Great Men Are Not Chosen President." The most important factor in his answer was that great men are generally not needed "in tranquil times" (Bryce, 1910:80). It may be that "Good-Time Charlie" governors emerged in part because states historically enjoyed tranquil times. But the new policy context presents governors with unique opportunities for effective policy leadership—leadership that can make a difference in the well-being of their states' citizens. Certainly, this new policy context is a worthy challenge for the best of a state's political talent. Certainly, too, this new policy context is the reason why great individuals ought now to be elected governor.

9 A NEW PROFESSIONALISM IN CITY MANAGEMENT

John Nalbandian

The field of city management, for a long time the mainstay of professionalism in public administration, finds itself going in a new direction. Once envisioned as politically neutral administrators, city managers have become policy advocates, negotiators of diverse community interests, and consensus builders. The evolution of their role speaks highly of their skills and stature in contemporary communities. But an uneasiness exists as managers shed the mantle of neutrality in the policy-making process, for in so doing, gradually they are disassociated from a supportive, yet evidently archaic, philosophical and intellectual heritage some seventy-five years old.

The changing role of the city manager is creating a crisis in legitimacy—a growing distance between the actual role of the manager and its idealization. Today, the idea of a politically neutral chief administrative officer lacks even theoretical credence. The role has evolved through necessity and perhaps expediency. The contemporary challenge facing those committed to professional administration of local governments requires searching for a new way to justify a visible role for nonelected municipal administrators based on our democratic heritage as well as today's political reality.

This chapter identifies new roots for city management grounded in the values and politics of today's communities. Built on this contemporary understanding, a new professionalism in city management is emerging. Managers must recognize more fully what is behind the challenge their profession faces.

Modern City Management

For several decades city management has been evolving in ways that challenge the traditional city manager's role. In 1985 Charldean Newell and

David N. Ammons (1987) conducted a nationwide survey of city managers in municipalities with over one hundred thousand population to identify the relative importance of various role expectations. In comparison with Deil Wright's (cited in Newell and Ammons, 1987) study conducted twenty years earlier, they found that 56 percent of the city managers they surveyed identified their policy-making role as most important compared to 22 percent in 1965.

Howard Tipton, city manager in Daytona Beach, provides a glimpse of the problems and activities a policy-oriented contemporary city manager faces in a dynamic economic environment. They include

> solicting proposals for a new convention center and headquarters hotel; negotiating for parking that will help existing business; working to secure a new anchor tenant for downtown; selling the need for a new harbor development that creates a drawing for redevelopment areas; negotiating for new city golf courses so as to improve community recreation and attract high quality residential development; convincing a developer to provide a free site for a new stadium and selling the old stadium site to a university for its expansion needs; packaging a low interest loan program with local bankers to facilitate the rehabilitation of downtown buildings; negotiating the purchase of key sites that accomplish redevelopment needs; negotiating with property owners outside the city to annex their property; negotiating interlocal agreements among local governments for provision of services or distribution of revenues; and lobbying state legislators. (1989:178)

John Dever, former city manager and past president of the International City Management Association, voices the frustration that frequently leads to active managerial involvement in policy making:

> A major project in a city today takes 7–12 years to plan, finance and realize. How do you get people who are only interested in the next election or how good they look today to participate in this process? This takes council courage and managerial courage—sacrifice—and some communities demand it. Some cities get it through leadership by the council, mayor, or managers—or a combination. The manager must provide whatever assistance is needed, if there is political leadership. If there is none, the manager must foster it—sometimes by taking the lead. (1987:19)

The challenges Tipton and Dever face require substantial technical expertise. But the expertise extends to an understanding of the politics, economics, and social dimensions of local government as well. Contemporary problems require a high level of managerial skill, problem-solving ability, interpersonal sensitivity, tolerance for ambiguity, and willingness to accept responsibility. Finally, they attract more community and intergovernmental interests into the local political arena than traditional city management envisioned.

In brief, contemporary city managers are entwined in the policy-making process; they respond to expectations from community interests and administrative staff as well as the governing body; and they find themselves balancing and compromising demands for efficiency with demands for political responsiveness.

City management has become a politically active profession even as it avoids partisan and electoral politics. Further, the most salient politics in today's communities involve policy processes and the relationship between politicians and bureaucrats and community interests rather than the formal dynamics of electoral processes.

Traditional Foundations of City Management

In contrast to this picture of the manager's role are beliefs which for seventy-five years have validated the manager's traditional position, providing the philosophical rationale for the council-manager form of government and for professionalism in city management. These beliefs are that the work of city administrators separates them from policy formulation; that the city manager is accountable to the governing body alone for policy direction; and that efficiency and political responsiveness can be harmoniously pursued in the community.

The Separation of Politics and Administration

Reform in local government at the turn of the century operated against a political backdrop unfamiliar to managers in most contemporary communities. Separation of legislative and executive powers was common, bicameral legislatures existed, and numerous administrative as well as political officials were elected. The watchword for the construction of governmental form was vigilance against the arrogation of power—the spirit in which the United States Constitution was born.

Efficiency suffered under these various forms of local government, which were built on the ideas of checks and balances and separation of powers. Machine politics grew, in part, as a vehicle allowing common citizens—a large number of them immigrants—to make their way through these governmental mazes and as a means for the legislature to coordinate or control the discretion of independently elected members of the executive branch (Goodnow, 1900:25).

To perpetuate themselves, political machines relied on personnel appointments through systems of spoils and through favoritism in the award of government contracts, franchises, purchasing, and licenses. In short, what we regard today as administrative processes, subject to the norms of impartiality and efficiency, were vehicles of self-interest and the currency of political exchange and coordination. Reformers believed that government had become corrupt. People sought office for self-interest, and inefficiency was common.

The reformers responded to corruption and inefficiency in two ways. First, they sought to remove politics from administrative processes. Second, they reduced administration to a technical field subject to rational analysis rather than politics.

In the reformer's ideal, politics and administration were separate yet connected spheres of action. Politics was concerned with policy making, while administration involved policy execution (Goodnow, 1900:5). Moreover, the essence of city government was seen as falling into the administrative sphere—providing services efficiently (Goodnow, 1900:84; Ridley and Nolting, 1934:2). Leonard White succinctly wrote, "The business of government in the twentieth century is fundamentally the business of administration" (1926:24). One year later, White wrote his book *The City Manager* (1927).

Further separating politics from administration was the reformers' view that efficient administrative processes and techniques could be discovered scientifically. As the scientific management movement grew in the early part of the century, this belief in scientific analysis and problem solving reached its peak. There was one best way to build sidewalks, sewers, bridges, and streets, and there was little room for politics in the process.

Removing politics from administration and placing the reins of administration into the hands of an administrative expert, whether accomplished in theory or practice, raised serious questions for those sensitive to democratic theory. How could the administrative arm of government be held accountable to the people if it was isolated and protected from political processes?

Administrative Accountability

The answer to the accountability question was creative and revolutionary. If power could be unified rather than divided into separate branches, it could be harnessed for public purposes.

The reformers sought to unify the power of the legislative and executive branches, arguing that all power should flow from the legislature (Childs,

1913, 1915). The executive who would be responsible for policy implementation and administrative processes would report to a small governing body that would restrict itself to questions of public policy. The legislative body, of course, would be accountable to the citizens through electoral processes. There would be no checks and balances; they would not be needed because the structure of government would not provide the executive with independent authority.

In addition to unifying power in the legislature, the reformers sought to consolidate administrative processes under a single executive position (Ridley and Nolting, 1934). If executives were not responsible for administrative processes, what good would it do to hold them accountable for such processes? The reformers solved this problem by advocating a short ballot and eliminating some offices that formerly had been subject to election and making them subject to appointment by the chief executive officer.

For the reformers, corrupt machine politics had dirtied politics so badly that reducing the impact of any form of politics on the city seemed positive. Few thought that chief executives might abuse the consolidated administrative power they possessed. After all, not only were chief administrative officers to be accountable to the governing body, theoretically they were politically neutral—experts in administration, "on tap and not on top."

Efficiency and the Public Interest

The idea that the chief administrative officer was an expert fit nicely with the emphasis on efficiency in the early part of the twentieth century. There was an unbridled faith in science and rationality which the scientific management movement captured (Waldo, 1948). Leonard White pointedly asserted that "the whole technical equipment of present day administration rests upon scientific achievement" (1926:14).

The emphasis on efficiency extended beyond the engineer's notion of input-output ratios. Efficiency was the opposite of corruption. According to Samuel Haber, "Efficiency and good came closer to meaning the same thing in these years than in any other period of American history" (1964:ix). How could anyone argue against efficiency in government when efficiency was seen as a moral good?

The business community, the symbol of efficiency, also was regarded positively. In contrast, the reformers identified politics as a source of corruption and inefficiency (Stone, Price, and Stone, 1940:27). If one separated the policy-making function from administrative functions, unified rather than separated power, and then consolidated administrative authority in a chief administrative officer, one could replicate the model of a business organization (Childs, 1913, 1965). Richard S. Childs deliberately adopted the title *city manager* to parallel the *general manager* descriptor common in business enterprise (Stone, Price, and Stone, 1940:11). For the reformers, in large measure, government was a business, and the value of efficiency should prevail both in the design of government structure and in administrative procedure.

The council-manager plan reflects most clearly the reformers' esteem for efficiency and their desire to depoliticize government.

Depoliticizing the City

Administratively, the city manager is seen as a professional—the administrative expert whose decisions are governed by managerial principles, scientific techniques, and rationality. Organizations, whether public or private, are regarded as machines and are subject to the same underlying principles of organization (Mooney, 1937; Urwick, 1937; Willoughby, 1927:ix). Luther Gulick and Lyndall Urwick's edited volume *Papers on the Science of Administration* (1937) reflects the "organization as machine" metaphor in many different ways. Like a machine, all the parts in an organization must work together. The presence of conflict indicates a breakdown, a deficiency. The key to administrative efficiency is coordination and singleness of purpose. Harmony signifies that all is well.

The council-manager form extends the depoliticization of government beyond administrative processes into the political sphere as well (Haber, 1964:chap. 6). Unifying powers rather than separating them reflects the assumption and creates the image of the community as a harmonious unit with a single purpose. This belief is reflected in the way the council-manager form structured elections. They would be nonpartisan, focusing on local issues rather than party labels and national politics. The governing body would be elected at large under the assumption that individuals still make a difference in government and that individuals with a communitywide perspective are better qualified to serve than those advocating a special interest or constituency. Even more basic was the belief that the community exists as a whole, not as a sum of interests.

Further indicating the deemphasis of politics is the idea that politics is a part-time endeavor in which political amateurs are the rule, not the exception. The chief administrative officer is charged with the day-to-day running of the government. The governing body is charged with establishing policy decisions and overseeing the city manager. The council-manager form envisions a governing body composed of a mayor selected by the governing body from its members—preferably business leaders—who work during the day and are willing to serve the community in repayment for their economic good fortune (Stone, Price, and Stone, 1940:pt. 3).

Vulnerability of the Council-Manager Plan

Almost immediately, weaknesses were found in the council-manager plan which foreshadowed the present crisis in legitimacy. Foremost among them was division over the role of the city manager, despite the rhetoric that the governing body made policy and the city manager implemented it.

Richard Childs, who conceived the manager plan, envisioned the manager as the council's expert "servant." According to Childs (1915), if the council is to be held responsible by the people "for every detail of the city management," it must be allowed to interfere in administration. Elsewhere, Childs (1916) suggests that a manager can only offer as good administration as the governing body is willing to take responsibility for. He believed that the only way managers could enact a neutral administrative role was if they posed no threat to the governing body and if they were seen as innocuous to the community at large.

This view was strongly debated among the first managers, who appeared more comfortable with action and maintaining their prerogatives as executives, and occasionally as reformers, than with reflection on democratic theory (White, 1927:182–98). Haber concludes, "On paper, the City Manager was a strict construction of Goodnow's maxims. However, in the most celebrated management municipalities, the manager soon eclipsed the elected council" (1964:104). In dialogue at the early conferences of city managers, Childs himself debated the role of the manager with those assembled, many of whom argued for and had taken on a more active, visible role in their communities. He expressed his concern about the moral advocates among the managers, whose verve seemed to have set them apart from their councils and the people they served. He said in this regard, "I am glad to see that most city managers see that . . . their function is to carry out the popular will as it is expressed to them, not to seek to oppose or to control the current of public opinion" (1916:103–4).

A second weakness discovered almost immediately had to do with the lack of political leadership on governing bodies, a contemporary concern as well. According to Leonard White, "One of the puzzling problems in connection with the city-manager position is presented by the difficulties in achieving trustworthy and competent political leadership" (1927:165). In part, the managers were more visible in their communities than Childs had expected they would be because there was no active political leadership to remind them of their role. White reports, "When the Republican national convention met in Cleveland in 1924 there was displayed over the city hall a large banner, 'Welcome to Cleveland, W. R. Hopkins, manager'" (1927:10). In their zeal to reduce the power of political machines, the reformers failed to acknowledge the legitimate role of politics in the community. White recognized that by advocating amateur politicians, the council-manager plan limited the likelihood that strong political leadership would emerge in governing bodies (1927:165).

A third weakness centers on the belief that efficiency and the public interest go hand in hand. A few of the early critics recognized that at-large elections, amateur politicians, and courting of the business community would leave many citizens feeling estranged from government, which previously had been as close as their block worker and precinct captain (Upson, 1915). Childs commented in this vein, pointing to elections in Dayton: "In Dayton there is extra danger in the fact that the business men at the beginning had things too wholly their own way and elected a handpicked business ticket. Now business men comprise but a trifling percentage of the population and live a good deal in a little social world of their own, and a good many currents of opinion can flow that business men know nothing of" (1915:120).

Early concerns with the plan were expressed over the tenure of managers. Today these weaknesses have spawned major concerns about the plan itself: the policy-making role of the manager and the reality of accountability mechanisms and the idea that efficiency and responsiveness are not always compatible.

The Challenge to Legitimacy of Council-Manager Government

Although these contemporary concerns are voiced in some communities and by some academicians, the conversation is not uncommon inside city management circles as well. For everyone who believes in council-manager government, even infrequent requests for information about a strong-mayor form invite anxiety—and justifiably so. The strong-mayor form symbolizes the target of yesterday's reformers. Today's anxiety is not prompted by potential job loss; it is associated with threat to an institution—the council-manager form of government.

Administration under Attack

City managers and the International City Management Association are justifiably concerned about attacks on the council-manager plan, yet the criticisms simply localize a broader debate. Government in general is under attack, and professionalism in particular suffers.

In the past several decades two major trends have occurred in society which fundamentally affect politics and ultimately our understanding of why people criticize the council-manager plan. First, government works, and therefore people have higher expectations and place more demands on it. People know their trash will be picked up, snow will be removed, streets will be repaired, water will be drinkable, and sewers will work. This is not always the case, but enough so that people expect more. If cities were unable to deliver services, citizens' expectations would not continue to grow. Elaine Sharp expresses the point: "The more the broad mass of the population is exposed to the problem-solving capacities of urban government's service-delivery bureaucracies, the more they develop a taste for these services which is incapable of satisfaction" (1986:173).

Related to Sharp's conclusion that effective service delivery stimulates higher expectations is the more general proposition that people know they can make a difference in their communities. It is not just through the initiative and referendum in California that citizens influence policy and politics. Nationwide, citizens exert significant pressure in rezoning cases, location of landfills, school curricula, and economic development.

Adding to these pressures is the observation that issues that used to fall under the umbrella of private transactions now have become public. The simplest example is the pressure to ban smoking. It used to be that smoking was an individual behavior governed by traditional norms. In part, because government works, as nonsmokers realized the costs of smoking, they turned smoking from a private activity into a collective one. And when they were effective, they unintentionally challenged government to legitimize to smokers why it was interfering in a private matter. Whether government requires motorcycle riders to wear helmets, prohibits smoking in public buildings, sanctions or prohibits abortions, subsidizes economic development, or provides sanitized needles to drug addicts, fundamental questions of legitimacy are raised. What is it we want our government to be and do?

While government comes under increasing pressure to justify itself, the ability of administrators and bureaucracies in general to do their work has advanced at a much faster rate than the ability of elected officials to do their work. Moreover, though it is far easier today to be an effective administrator than to be an effective politician, the importance of politics has not diminished.

Further, solving problems requires so much reliance on expertise and rational analysis that the importance of bureaucracies will not diminish in the future. Therefore, the gap between effective politics and administration will increase, not decrease.

More effective politics, not more profressionalism, is needed to improve the legitimacy of government. Nevertheless, professionalism will grow simply because of the nature of problems faced by the society. The broad problem is that as the power of professionals is increasing, their authority is decreasing (Schaar, 1969:126). This is because effective administration, as we presently conceive of it, cannot overcome ineffective politics. Furthermore, in the absence of effective politics, the downside of administration is accentuated.

Professionals think rationally, and objectively, and in some cases scientifically. As John Schaar writes, "Any bureaucrat who based his decisions upon conscience, trained prudence, intuition, dreams, empathy, or even common sense and personal experience would be *ipso facto* guilty of malfeasance" (1969:121). Schaar's coup de grace is "If you were to assign the task of devising a religion to a bureaucracy, you could say beforehand that the product would be all law and no prophesy, all rule and no revelation" (1969:120). As important as professionalism is, it cannot answer fundamental questions of individual worth, pride in belonging, and the relationship of citizens to their institutions.

In their own ways I think that citizens and elected officials know this better than the broad array of professionals who work for city governments or governments at any other level. Perhaps the uneasiness that some citizens and elected officials feel in their conversations and relationships with professionals is an uneasiness they feel in their own lives as citizens dealing with professionals.

A New Foundation for Professionalism in Local Government

The critique of bureaucracy becomes focused on local government because, compared to state and federal government, its scope and complexity turn these broad concerns about professionalism into specific and identifiable issues. Specific actors and settings unfortunately deflect our attention away from these broader issues, which face contemporary professionals in local government. In so doing, they preclude the broad understanding necessary for lasting solutions.

If we are to lay a new theoretical foundation to legitimize the power of professionals in local government, we must accept the observation that there is no indication that the quality of politics in our communities is going to improve. Recognizing the importance of politics to the legitimacy of administration, how does the professional proceed? The first step is recognizing that politics is about community values, and if professionalism cannot be legitimated within the confines of the city council, it must turn to the community itself for legitimacy.

The difficulty the professional faces is that community values and professional values—as presently constructed—often do not coincide. The reason, of course, is that elected officials are supposed to provide the link between the analytical perspective of professional staff and the representational interests in the community.

We start laying the new foundation by portraying the community in terms of values and focusing on political responsiveness. This term, the most important in democratic theory, is now devoid of meaning because it is used to justify anything an elected official does. As part of a new beginning, I suggest that responsiveness should be measured according to four other values which are in concert fundamental to our political culture. Further, I will suggest that any community can be viewed from this value perspective, and each community will place a different emphasis on each of the values so that each community has a distinct political profile.

The first such value is representativeness, the idea that public officials represent the demands of citizens, groups of citizens, and special interests. Demands from citizens are weighed against other demands and against priorities to determine if they are to be met. Fundamental to the value of representation is debate over the means by which various interests will be articulated in policy-making venues. For example, minority citizens in many contemporary communities criticize council-manager government for its emphasis on at-large elections, which favor majority interests, over district elections, which favor minority representation.

Thomas Downs, a longtime city manager and current president of the Triborough Bridge Authority in New York City, reflects the value of representativeness in city management when he characterizes politics as "complex, messy and conflict oriented." He elaborates: "The more diverse the councils are, the more I like working in that environment. I like the diversity. I think it is part of the normal, healthy city process. Cities are complex, messy, and conflict oriented. They are melting pots. The more diverse the city council is, the more diverse the politics. They probably better represent the real city. So, it is easier, in some respects, to deal with real problems" (1987:34).

Downs's comments take the profession further away from how the original city managers—drawn largely from the ranks of civil engineers—might think about a problem. How does one extract a problem from a "melting pot?" How do bureaucracies process through administrative routine problems extracted from a melting pot?

The second value, efficiency, encompasses rational and objective analysis of public problems, cost-benefit analysis, objectivity, and, generally speaking, bureaucratic norms and professionalism. Jack Manahan, director of finance in Johnson County, Kansas, articulates the value of efficiency when he says: "Importance must be continually given to technical competence. City managers must continue to be technically competent so they can continue to make strong recommendations to the council. Managers can't become yes men and just look for the majority. Consensus building is important, but not above everything else. Local government managers have to push their councils to make the right decisions" (interview, April 20, 1986).

The value of individual rights connotes legal protection and is expressed when property owners request rezoning, public employees invoke merit system or constitutional protection, and clients of public services seek redress for inequitable treatment. The more that the lives of citizens are affected by government, the more likely citizens will be to seek protection from government decisions they perceive as capricious and arbitrary. That is, the more powerful the administrative instruments of government become, the more emphasis subjects of that power will place on rights to public notice, hearings, and due process (Rosenbloom, 1987, 1988).

Stewart Margolis (1988), a resident of Inglewood, California, expressed the value of individual rights in a letter to the *Los Angeles Times*:

> Rent control is not just impractical or unfairly implemented—it is morally wrong. Property rights are among the most basic rights that all humans have. When the government steps in and tells people what to do with their property (i.e., how much rent they can charge) it violates those rights. It doesn't matter if the majority of voters approve the action. The United States is a constitutional democracy where our freedoms and rights cannot be voted away. That is what distinguishes us from Nazi Germany or the Soviet Union—or at least it used to.

The last value, social equity, is the most controversial. Social equity as a concept is very similar to the idea of distributive justice but with an important difference. Distributive justice is equally relevant in assessing the distribution of public services to individuals or groups. But fairness frequently is calculated on the basis of the distribution of goods and services to groups, not individuals (Hero, 1986). The term *social* in the value social equity implies that the unit of analysis is a group or a group characteristic rather than an individual, and it distinguishes social equity from individual rights. The term *equity* implies some calculation of fairness, right, or justice.

There are numerous examples in municipal government which demonstrate the attention this controversial value commands. As an illustration, following a tax increase in 1970, Kansas City provided free trash bags for its citizens (representation). In 1988, however, a projected revenue shortfall stimulated the city manager to propose eliminating distribution of free trash bags (efficiency). Amid protests from citizens, a new plan (reflecting the social equity value) emerged that would make people on food stamps, welfare, Aid to the Blind, and Supplemental Security Income still eligible for free bags.

In Los Angeles County a plan to eliminate public sudsidy of private hospital emergency rooms was countered with the argument that it would have a disproportionate impact on the "sickest and poorest" residents. In Dallas, Deputy Mayor Pro Tem Diane Ragsdale criticized a plan to raise fees at city swimming pools. She said, "People on the bottom of the economic ladder cannot stretch any farther to afford basic services the city should provide, like swimming pools" (Housewright, 1988). In San Francisco, the planned closing of an unprofitable Wells Fargo Bank in the inner city drew attention to the effect the corporate decision would have on minority communities.

To summarize, in city management political responsiveness equals representativeness plus efficiency plus individual rights plus social equity. All communities will reflect these four values, but not in the same proportions. Sometimes these values will reinforce one another, and when they do, very strong public policies will emerge. In most cases, they will conflict, and compromise policies will result. In addition, community value profiles change over time so that at one point a community may place more value on representativeness (politics) and at another time on efficiency (professionalism).

If councils fail to provide political leadership, either because they are unable or unwilling, the values of representativeness and social equity, legislative values, will not enter public debate as forcefully as they should. In such a case, the legitimacy of administration, if not its power, depends upon the incorporation of these values into administrative processes. Further, to the extent that individual rights forcefully affect public policy processes, their importance in administrative action as well cannot be underestimated. In short, if a governing body does not embody the community's values, the legitimacy of professionalism depends on it successfully doing so.

Adopting the values perspective on professionalism in city management may appear idealistic, but the profession is naturally evolving in that direction, and illustrations of its effectiveness may be found throughout the country. The essence of these changes is reflected in administrative processes which at one time were isolated from pubic scrutiny but now are characterized by much more citizen involvement (Sharp, 1986; Thomas, 1986:chap. 7). For example, Michael Gleason, city manager in Eugene, Oregon, reported on a process that focuses community values on budgetary activities (personal communication, November 1, 1989, January 10, 1990). In the classic council-manager plan, staff prepares an executive budget which the manager submits to the council for review and approval. In Eugene, relevant portions of the manager's executive budget are routed through appropriate boards and commissions before they become the focus of a public hearing. Then the manager transmits the budget to a public committee appointed by the city council. The public body, which includes council members, reviews the budget and submits its recommendation to the city council, which holds another hearing. The city council may alter the recommended budget by 10 percent.

Gleason indicates that in 1988, thirty-two meetings were required before the budget was adopted in Eugene. A lot of staff time is spent on budget preparation because the public committee is not as knowledgeable as the council members, and they need to be presented with material they can understand. At the same time, staff work sheets are developed in detail in anticipation of questions about individual line items which council members familiar with the budget process might simply defer to staff. Gleason returns to the budget committee and city council quarterly to reconcile the estimated budget with the actual budget.

The operation of some fifty-five boards and commissions involving some five hundred citizens in Eugene also provides examples of how administrative aspects of government are increasingly influenced by citizen involvement. According to Gleason, it is the manager's formal responsibility to promulgate rules, regulations, and fees involving the airport. In practice, however, staff develops administrative proposals which are forwarded to the Airport Commission for review. The commission then recommends the proposal to the city manager, who authorizes a public hearing and then the appropriate rule or regulation. In effect, the Airport Commission becomes an adviser to administrative staff as well as a channel for policy and budgetary proposals that will be brought before the city council.

The advisory role of the boards and commissions places a significant number of citizens in an intermediate position between their private lives and election to office or public employment. The boards and commissions are training grounds for future council members. Further, the city council demonstrates sensitivity to the values of representativeness and social equity in its appointments. Gleason points out that the city maintains a personnel system that focuses on the demographic characteristics of the boards and commissions and includes a training program for new appointees.

The pervasive role of these boards and commissions has not only affected the administrative work of staff, it also has influenced the criteria used to make staff appointments. According to Gleason, it is essential that department heads be able and willing to work with these boards and commissions and neighborhood groups. Gleason recruits and selects department heads with this orientation in mind and then evaluates their work with these groups. Further, he does not staff these boards and commissions with junior employees.

Consequences

Of the many consequences of the approach I am proposing, I will point out two. First, I am suggesting that professionalism in city management must focus on process, not outcomes. City management is about the creation of culture in a community, not about the design of that culture. Further, whatever activities are required to create that culture must be nested in the end values. In other words, the process of searching for the design of the community's value profile must be based on the same values that are anticipated. If a city is searching for its perspective on social equity, the search must reflect social equity. Similarly, if the community is searching for a meaning of representativeness, it must employ representative means and bodies. In other words, the value searched for must be embodied in the search.

The second point is that throughout this chapter I have deliberately spoken of professionals generally as well as city managers specifically. I believe that effective city managers are already incorporating the values of representativeness, efficiency, individual rights, and social equity into administrative processes. But I would argue that the legitimacy of the city manager position depends on the view of professionalism more broadly held in the community. In this sense, city managers are at the mercy of their department heads, who interact frequently with elected officials and citizens. For example, I am struck by the transformation in recent years of the parks and recreations function (Bannon, 1987). With the increased use by citizens of private fitness facilities, recreation programs in many municipalities have become social services. Now, recreation directors must develop programs which the community wants (representativeness), pay their way through fees (efficiency), ensure that programs are available equally to all segments of the community (social equity), and ensure that the programs do not create legal risks for the municipality (individual rights).

As municipal staffs become more professional, I become concerned for the city manager, especially because common wisdom has developed that city managers take care of external relations while the assistant city manager takes care of internal city operations. What department of city government is solely concerned with internal operations? As the legitimacy of city management grows to depend on recognition of community values, the difference between internal and external city operations decreases in importance. Although city managers are commonly seen today as brokers, negotiators, and consensus builders in the community, similar roles internally cannot go unattended. The key word is *legitimacy,* and this connotes community.

CONCLUSION

William H. Stewart and
Robert B. Denhardt

This volume of essays rests on the belief so ably expounded upon by Coleman B. Ransone that public leadership is worth thinking and writing about. As the reader probably has observed, however, the reasons for studying executive leadership, as reflected in the preceding chapters, are as varied as the backgrounds of the scholars and educators whose contributions are presented in this volume. Still, in each we see something of the commitment of the late Professor Ransone to expanded knowledge and rigorous practice as essential to effective leadership. Also, as noted in the Introduction, Coleman Ransone stressed the importance of the relationship of the public leader to the public with whom she or he participates in the governing process. This concern has been expressed in the preceding essays. At this point, let us briefly attempt to integrate these and several other major themes and issues developed by our authors.

It is hoped that some of these essays will be incorporated into the reading lists of leadership education programs. Like Ransone in stressing the need for instruction in leadership, Charles Goodsell suggests that "higher standards of professional conduct in all executive leaders" may be the result of reflective education. He feels further that, with appropriate effort, specific standards, perhaps emerging from leadership studies, are attainable "and should be met in public service leadership."

The Need for Knowledgeable Leaders

Donald Wells, who spotlights state governors in his essay, sees a shifting state policy environment. Indeed, in his view, "the policy environment within the state[s] has changed dramatically." This modified environment means that leaders need to have different characteristics than in the past. Even though he finds evolution to be in the direction of much greater complexity, he still feels that the individuals needed as leaders can, if sufficiently knowledgeable, provide the guidance demanded in the area of public policy.

There are many new opportunities for leadership, according to Wells. The area of waste disposal was perhaps the most critical he cited as requiring more brainpower. Leaders will have to have much more aptitude and much broader perspectives in this policy field and others, he perceives, because the major problems confronting us today are not only of contemporary concern but "have intergenerational significance." The point is that complex problems require knowledgeable leadership. In his essay, William Stewart points to some of the consequences of a lack of informed leadership, a condition that may be worsened when operative patterns of intergovernmental relations obstruct rather than facilitate joint public problem-solving efforts.

George Frederickson says that we should pay careful attention to the "intellect, views on the issues, [and potential] capacity to affect the general good" of persons in or considered for positions in the public service. For Frederickson, public leadership is synonymous with the "public spirit at work." Robert Denhardt and Kevin Prelgovisk stressed the need for a broadly diffused and much "improved capacity for human beings to exert leadership," which, they further observe, "inevitably involves ethics and morals," as well as cognitive knowledge.

Leaders as Policy Makers

Some of our writers have focused generally on leadership while others have studied leadership in various arenas in which individual enterprise is most frequently encountered. All of the authors, however, give at least some attention to leaders as policy makers.

In state government, Deil Wright and Cheryl Miller, Wells, and Stewart find numerous new and important currents relating to policy making. The first two authors target shifts in the character, content, and context of gubernatorial leadership over the past two decades. Wright and Miller also comment on "changes in legislative capacities and capabilities [which have] had [an impact] on state administration." They establish that legislatures now perform "a broader role in overseeing policy execution"—a role that is more or less ongoing and not so episodic as it was previously.

Ryan Barilleaux observes that at the apex of the leadership system, the presidency, the chief executive does a lot of "vicarious policy making"— that is, the president leads through others. Thus there is a need for widely disseminated leadership capabilities. Barilleaux and Whicker and Areson point to numerous changes in presidential leadership. Barilleaux demonstrates the value (from a leadership perspective) of examining the nature and practice of contemporary presidential leadership and the distinguishing features of what he names the "postmodern presidency." The writers believe that not only in the presidential arena but elsewhere as well, there has been a diffusion of leadership opportunities in recent years. This makes the studies of executive leadership developed by the commentators here that much more timely.

In his overview of the American intergovernmental system, Stewart sees trends in recent years in the direction of the wider distribution of leadership freedom. Stewart finds competing models of operational federalism to be important to the wider exercise of public leadership, especially in state and local arenas. Different patterns or models of intergovernmental relations allow for varying kinds and amounts of leadership.

As is the case with other scholars, Stewart sees increasing agreement with the proposition that Washington is not "all-wise." Thus there is a strong need to bolster independent—and/or interdependent—decision-making capabilities outside the Capitol. Detached leadership initiatives are needed, not only strong intergovernmental partnerships. Stewart's evidence persuades him to conclude that there has been and continues to be a diffusion of leadership opportunities—not simply because this is an attractive model of federalism but because a large, complex federal system indisputably requires such. Heavy-handed centralization is not essential for positive responses to public problems and surely would be counterproductive.

Though he accentuates recognition of a much wider sharing of leadership responsibilities within the American federal system, Stewart also points to potential and actual problems with "usurpation," with an inappropriate arrogation of leadership roles, as when members of Congress attempt to function de facto as city council members. Wells, however, is not too disturbed about alleged attempts of federal officials to micromanage what is going on in state and local arenas because he finds that already "public policy in the United States is remarkably state-centered." In Wells's view, the "nationalization of the states" hypothesis should not be regarded as proven fact. Instead, he is convinced that it would be more accurate to speak of the "localization and regionalization of national policy objectives" because of the diffusion of policy leadership. Indeed, as he explores what is going on in the states, Wells sees "a pervasive revitalization of state activity in the area of public policy." Further, Wells sees more benefits in the competition for leadership among national, state, and local authorities than Stewart apparently does.

The survey data reported by Wright and Miller show that in most instances devaluing of locally staffed positions is unwise because there are more people available for leadership outside Washington than at any previous time. State bureaucracies are performing more diverse functions than ever before, according to Wright and Miller, in an increasingly large number of spheres of activity. State movement in many of these areas has been strongly encouraged by federal aid so Wright and Miller also examine and report on important findings on the impact of the receipt of federal aid on executive leadership and administrative accountability. Their data give renewed life to the old hypothesis that federal aid distorts state and local spending choices. These writers also find that intragovernmental oversight, particularly state legislative oversight of state administration, has become much more important in recent years. They identify this phenomenon as "simultaneous accountability."

Public Leadership as Professional Leadership

Coleman Ransone educated women and men for professional leadership positions in the federal government as well as in state and local governments through the Southern Regional Training Program. We believe that this volume of essays is stronger because of the blend of national and subnational, public and private, and abstract and specific perspectives it features. Some chapters focus on leadership in the most visible arenas (e.g., the presidency) while others exhibit more interest in arenas most of the time only minimally in the public view (e.g., a local staff agency strongly subsidized with federal funds). One or more of the essayists are concerned with public leadership at all levels of society.

Nevertheless, despite this diversity of concentration, there seems to be agreement with Ransone among all of the writers who address the subject that public administration is a profession and that broadly trained public administration professionals are needed in all arenas of public life. From the standpoint of the scholar and theory builder, most have some confidence that, with rigorous analysis, it will be possible at some point in the future to identify "generalizable principles, motifs, and lessons for . . . leadership and public policy" (quoting from Wells). Meanwhile, they seek to give greater clarity to the notion of public leadership, feeling that, as the expression is now used, it is too vague and too ambiguous, both as an activity and as a profession.

Different authors stress different requirements of successful professional leadership. In Goodsell's view, professional influence consists of "a set of values on the part of executive leaders which can be regarded as a higher form of professionalism." Frederickson defines his view of professional leadership as "the effective operation of government agencies coupled with a structured pattern of interaction with the public to improve the common good."

Activist Public Leadership

It is obvious from even the most cursory reading of the essays in this volume that our authors view the subject of professional leadership from an active rather than a passive perspective. Fundamentally, in Wells's view, those who would be leaders need to have a "commit[ment] to making a difference" in the quality of public life. In an age of cynicism regarding the positive uses of government, Goodsell underscores the requirement that political professionals believe in "the ability to use government to make a difference in people's lives, an ability possessed by no one else" but public leaders. In his incisive analysis of the evolution of professional city management, John Nalbandian shows how the original idea that city managers were to be relatively passive professionals very soon proved to be unworkable.

As important as it is to get a better grasp on what public leadership is, it is also necessary to know what it is not. Several of our authors have very definite ideas on this subject. For Frederickson, public administration is more than just "government administration." Because he defines public so broadly, for him, public leadership "does not simply mean leadership in government." Frederickson is also careful to distinguish between the leadership he envisions and what he refers to as "careerism and individualism." Frederickson says that the kind of leadership that he seeks to promote involves much more than "avoiding doing evil."

Denhardt and Prelgovisk also approach the subject of leadership from a general perspective and take pains to distinguish true public leadership from inferior substitutes. Thus "cognitive knowledge alone is insufficient" to comprehend the qualities needed by the public leader. Articulating further their notion of the activist leader, Denhardt and Prelgovisk stress why more than affective proficiency is needed. Their contemporary leader will be involved in more than "the [merely] instrumental pursuit of established interests." An orientation toward the status quo could amount to simply "private management" and the manipulation of "institutionalized mechanisms for control." Public leadership must be more than this.

Continuing in this vein but in a specific leadership context, Barilleaux urges a new president "not to be [so] overwhelmed by a governing system and a political environment that [have] many centers of power" that she or he becomes merely an apologist for things as they are.

The Limitations of Leadership

Although the writers here are convinced of the need for executive leadership, none sees it as a panacea for all current ills. For example, Nalbandian, after his study of professional leadership in local affairs, concludes that "more effective politics, not more professionalism, is needed to improve the legitimacy of government." Frederickson, too, despite his stress on sharing leadership opportunities with the public (which warrants further reiteration), still feels it is necessary to recognize a "sharp decline in the ability [both] of the public at large [and] public agencies to act authoritatively."

Partly in response to enfeebling environmental conditions, Denhardt and Prelgovisk see "a failure of leadership throughout society." Wright and Miller, in interpreting their state-level data, see "no strong or consistent pro-[leadership] trends." "Stable status" is about the most optimistic interpretation that they can make of their data. This is because, according to these authors, "executive government has not produced heightened oversight . . . or the expected rise in . . . accountability." In the state gubernatorial arena, Miller and Wright view with some apprehension the situation in which governors' managerial activity is increasing but policy leadership is decreasing. This suggests a diminution of leadership. In his intergovernmental essay, Stewart finds conflicts, actual as well as potential, between politicians and "professional" administrators in multiple governmental arenas.

Wells feels the situation may not get much better in the near future because public leadership positions may "not appeal to the best potential leaders." At the national level, Whicker and Areson are forced to regard as merely conjectural whether "future presidents will be able to meet the nation's needs." Wells feels that one cause of the failure of effective national policy is excessive timidity in the face of well-organized interest groups. This is one of the causes of "policy paralysis at the national level." Though Wells finds much good in policy noncentralization, he points out that the "localization and regionalization of national policy objectives" may have negative implications for the exercise of presidential leadership. From an intragovernmental viewpoint, the president, for example, may now possess in law a "greater capacity for controlling executive branch policy making," but in other respects there are diminished resources with which to do so.

The Public in Public Leadership

Most of the essayists whose ideas were described above seem primarily concerned with possibilities for as well as limitations on official leadership. Some of the authors also have expressed an equally strong concern for enlarged opportunities for members of the public generally to help deal with "expensive, complex, and intractable" problems as well as to use and perfect their own leadership skills.

Early on in this volume, Frederickson stresses his concern that "we have virtually no elaboration of the word *public* in public administration." Working on this problem is critical, however, because Frederickson believes that official leaders alone cannot resolve the problems of "moral ambiguity," which stand in the way of an accurate perception of what is really in the public interest.

Nalbandian, who focused primarily on problems of city management, maintains that public involvement is needed "to legitimize the power of professionals in local government." Without fairly broad-based public participation, professionals will be governing spuriously. Nalbandian insists that a vital part of education for local leadership is sensitizing local leaders to "the values of representativeness and social equity" as aspects of public debate.

Again, in addition to cognitive knowledge, as Denhardt and Prelgovisk demonstrate, "strong consultative skills" are needed by all who would be leaders. This will involve "the ability to integrate many differing but complementary ideas." A strong commitment is also needed to other aspects of the group process. Indeed, in their view, it is impossible to discuss leadership without this critical element. Thus in addition to the admonition to "know thyself!" these writers urge, "know others!" Denhardt and Prelgovisk think that the best way to understand a particular exercise of leadership is as "an act of social development."

Denhardt and Prelgovisk particularly encourage us not to regard leadership roles, whether official or amateur, as set in concrete. These authors point out that leadership "shifts from person to person and from group to group over time." As Frederickson does, they underscore the public in "*public* leadership," that is, leadership that pursues interests which are "publicly defined in an open and evolving relationship." Wells believes that the public will insist on being involved, whether officially designated leaders like it or not. He quotes approvingly Fischhoff's finding that there is an "increasing [public] assertiveness about risk issues." For these and other reasons he enumerates, a very open policy "enactment process" is needed.

The public wants dialogue, Whicker and Areson believe, with leaders who have confidence that governmental institutions can be used to resolve important public problems. Thus presidents, like other leaders, must understand the policy environment, including "culture-based sentiment," so that true communication with the public can be established and maintained. Whicker and Areson's case studies point up the need to involve the presidential "audience" in the decision-making process. Presidential failure typically occurs when the president fails to consult with the public.

Final Thoughts

It would be naive to suggest that our authors, despite the perspicacity of their essays, have been able to resolve many of the tensions inherent in the analyses of public leadership which have been pursued in this volume. More valuably, the writers have clearly identified some of the more important sources of tension in their respective areas of study. One source of tension regarding public leadership, however, identified years ago by Coleman Ransone, may have been partially remedied by our authors. Wells notes Ransone's worry that there had been a lot of "research" but not much "reflection" in this area of study. These essays appear to contain ample quantities of each. They also seem to have struck an appropriate balance between the tendency (as identified by Goodsell) to be overly descriptive and confine one's interests to describing executive leadership or overly prescriptive in positing an ideal for executive leadership without a clear understanding of the empirical foundations of the normative model. This volume of essays also seems to have struck a reasonable balance between leadership in the abstract and the focus on particular leaders and groups of the led in specific power centers. We may now commend them to their readers in the exemplary spirit of the scholar, teacher, and friend to whom they are most respectfully dedicated.

REFERENCES

Abney, Glenn, and Thomas P. Lauth. 1983. "The Governor as Chief Administrator." *Public Administration Review* 43 (January–February): 40–49.

Adelman, Kenneth. 1984–85. "Arms Control with and without Agreements." *Foreign Affairs* 63 (Winter): 240–63.

Agresto, John. 1984. *The Supreme Court and Constitutional Democracy*. Ithaca, N.Y.: Cornell University Press.

Allen, Robert S., ed. 1949. *Our Sovereign State*. New York: Vanguard Press.

Alter, Jonathan. 1988. "How the Media Blew It." *Newsweek* (November 21): 24, 26.

Anderson, Martin. 1988. *Revolution*. San Diego: Harcourt Brace Jovanovich.

Anon. 1980. "The Overloaded System." *National Civic Review* (June): 301–6.

Bacharach, Peter, and Morton S. Baratz. 1970. *Poverty*. New York: Holt, Rinehart and Winston.

Ball, Howard. 1984. *Controlling Regulatory Sprawl*. Westport, Conn.: Greenwood Press.

Bannon, Joseph J., ed. 1987. *Current Issues in Leisure Services: Looking Ahead in a Time of Transition*. Washington, D.C.: ICMA.

Barber, Bernard. 1963. "Some Problems in the Sociology of the Professions." In *The Professions in America*, ed. Kenneth S. Lynn, pp. 15–34. Boston: Beacon Press.

Barber, James David. 1980. *The Pulse of Politics: Electing Presidents in the Media Age*. New York: Norton.

———. 1985. *Presidential Character*. 3d ed. Englewood Cliffs, N.J.: Prentice-Hall.

Barilleaux, Ryan J. 1986. "Executive Non-Agreements, Arms Control, and the Executive-Congressional Struggle in Foreign Affairs." *World Affairs*, no. 148 (Fall): 217–28.

———. 1988. *The Post-Modern Presidency*. New York: Praeger.

Bellah, Robert N., et al. 1985. *Habits of the Heart: Individualism and Commitment in American Life*. Berkeley and Los Angeles: University of California Press.

Bennis, Warren. 1976. *The Unconscious Conspiracy: Why Leaders Can't Lead*. New York: AMACOM.

———. 1983. "The Artform of Leadership." In *The Executive Mind*, ed. Suresh Srivastva, pp. 15–24. San Francisco: Jossey-Bass.

Bennis, Warren, and Burt Nanus. 1985. *Leaders: The Strategies for Taking Charge*. New York: AMACOM.

Bernick, E. Lee. 1979. "Gubernatorial Tools: Formal vs. Informal." *Journal of Politics* 41 (February): 656–64.

Beyle, Thad L. 1983. "Governors." In *Politics in the American States: A Comparative Analysis*, ed. Herbert L. Jacob and Kenneth N. Vines, pp. 207–37. 4th ed. Boston: Little, Brown.

———. 1985. *Gubernatorial Transitions: The 1982 Election*. Durham, N.C.: Duke University Press.

———. 1988. "The Institutionalized Powers of the Governorship: 1965–1985." *Comparative State Politics Newsletter* 9 (February): 23–29.

Beyle, Thad L., and Lynn R. Muchmore, eds. 1983. *Being Governor: A View from the Office*. Durham, N.C.: Duke University Press.

Beyle, Thad L., and J. Oliver Williams. 1972. *The American Governor in Behavioral Perspective*. New York: Harper & Row.

Bozeman, Barry. 1987. *All Organizations Are Public*. San Francisco: Jossey-Bass.

Brooks, Glen E. 1961. *When Governors Convene: The Governors Conference and National Politics*. Baltimore: Johns Hopkins University Press.

Bryce, James. 1910. *The American Commonwealth*. Vol. 1. New York: Macmillan.

Burns, James MacGregor. 1978. *Leadership*. New York: Harper & Row.

———. 1984. *The Power to Lead*. New York: Simon and Schuster.

Caraley, Demetrios. 1986. "Changing Conceptions of Federalism." *Political Science Quarterly* 101: 289–306.

Cavanaugh, Thomas E., and James L. Sundquist. 1985. "The New Two-Party System." In *The New Direction in American Politics*, ed. John E. Chubb and Paul E. Peterson, pp. 33–68. Washington, D.C.: Brookings Institution.

Childs, Richard S. 1913. "The Theory of the New Controlled Executive Plan." In *City Manager Plan of Government*, ed. Edward C. Mabie (1918), pp. 77–84. New York: Wilson Company. Reprinted from *National Municipal Review* 2 (January): 76–81.

———. 1915. "How the Commission-Manager Plan Is Getting Along." In *City Manager Plan of Government*, ed. Edward C. Mabie (1918), pp. 111–23. New York: Wilson Company. Reprinted from *National Municipal Review* 4 (July): 371–82.

———. 1965. *The First 50 Years of the Council-Manager Plan of Municipal Government*. New York: National Municipal League.

Childs, Richard S., Henry M. Waite, et al. 1916. "Professional Standards and Professional Ethics in the New Profession of City Manager." In *City Manager Plan of Government*, ed. Edward C. Mabie (1918), pp. 84–104. Reprinted from *National Municipal Review* 5 (April): 195–200.

Choi, Yearn Hong. 1984. "Issues of New Federalism in Low-Level Radioactive Waste Management: Cooperation or Confusion?" *State Government* 57: 13–20.

———. 1985. "Federalism and the Bias for Centralization." In *The New Direction in American Politics*, ed. John E. Chubb and Paul E. Peterson, pp. 273–306. Washington, D.C.: Brookings Institution.

Chubb, John E., and Paul E. Peterson, eds. 1985. *The New Direction in American Politics*. Washington, D.C.: Brookings Institution.

Citizens Conference on State Legislatures. 1971a. *The Sometime Governments: A Critical Study of 50 American Legislatures*. New York: Bantam Books.

———. 1971b. *State Legislatures: An Evaluation of Their Effectiveness: The Complete Report by the Citizens Conference on State Legislatures*. New York: Praeger.

Cleveland, Harlan. 1985. *The Knowledge Executive*. New York: E. P. Dutton.

Conlan, Timothy J., and Steven L. Abrams. 1981. "Federal Intergovernmental Regulation: Symbolic Politics in the New Congress." *Intergovernmental Perspective* 7 (Summer): 19–26.

Connolly, W. B., ed. 1984. *Legitimacy and the Modern State*. New York: New York University Press.

Corwin, Edward S. 1950. "The Passing of Dual Federalism." *Virginia Law Review* 36 (February): 1–24.

Cronin, Thomas E. 1980. *The State of the Presidency*. 2d ed. Boston: Little, Brown.

Denhardt, Robert B. 1981. *In the Shadow of Organization*. Lawrence: Regents Press of Kansas.

———. 1984. *Theories of Public Organization*. Monterey: Brooks/Cole.

———. 1987. "Action Skills in Public Administration." In *The Revitalization of the Public Service*, ed. Denhardt and Edward T. Jennings, pp. 119–32. Columbia: Department of Public Administration, University of Missouri.

Destler, I. M. 1981. "National Security II: The Rise of the Assistant." In *The Illusion of Presidential Government*, ed. Hugh Heclo and Lester M. Salamon, pp. 263–85. Boulder, Colo.: Westview.

Dever, Jeff. 1987. *Reflections of Local Government Professionals*, ed. John Nalbandian and Raymond G. Davis, pp. 13–19. Lawrence: Department of Public Administration, University of Kansas.

Dewey, John. 1954. *The Public and Its Problems*. Chicago: Swallow Press.

Divine, Robert A., ed. 1981. *Exploring the Johnson Years*. Austin: University of Texas Press.

Dometrius, Nelson C. 1979. "Measuring Gubernatorial Power." *Journal of Politics* 41 (February): 589–610.

Downs, Anthony. 1967. *Inside Bureaucracy*. Boston: Little, Brown.

Downs, Thomas. 1987. *Reflections of Local Government Professionals*, ed. John Nalbandian and Raymond G. Davis, pp. 21–38. Lawrence: Department of Public Administration, University of Kansas.

Dubnick, Mel, and Alan Gitelson. 1981. "Nationalizing State Policies." In *The Nationalization of the States*, ed. Jerome J. Hanus, pp. 39–74. Lexington, Mass.: Lexington Books.

Edelman, Murray. 1974. "The Politics of Persuasion." In *Choosing the President*, ed. James David Barber, pp. 149–73. Englewood Cliffs, N.J.: Prentice-Hall.

Edwards, George C. III. 1980. *Presidential Influence in Congress*. San Francisco: Freeman.

———. 1983. *The Public Presidency: The Pursuit of Popular Support*. New York: St. Martin's Press.

Edwards, George C. III, and Stephen J. Wayne. 1985. *Presidential Leadership: Politics and Policy Making*. New York: St. Martin's Press.

Elazar, Daniel J. 1966. *American Federalism: A View from the States*. New York: Thomas Crowell.

Ferguson, Charles E. 1971. *The Neoclassical Theory of Production and Distribution*. Cambridge: Cambridge University Press.

Fiedler, Fred E., and Joseph E. Garcia. 1987. *New Approaches to Effective Leadership*. New York: Wiley.

Fischhoff, Baruch. 1985. "Managing Risk Perception." *Issues in Science and Technology* 2: 83–96.

Fishel, Jeff. 1985. *Presidents and Promises*. Washington, D.C.: CQ Press.

Fisher, Louis. 1985. *Constitutional Conflicts between Congress and the Presidency*. Princeton: Princeton University Press.

Flathman, Richard E. 1966. *The Public Interest: An Essay Concerning the Normative Discourses of Politics*. New York: Wiley.

Franklin, Daniel Paul. 1987. "War Powers in the Modern Context." *Congress and the Presidency* 14 (Spring): 77–92.

Freeman, Frank H., Robert A. Gregory, and Miriam B. Clark. 1986. *Leadership Education: A Source Book*. Greensboro, N.C.: Center for Creative Leadership.

Gardner, John. 1984. *Excellence*. New York: Norton.

———. 1987. "Remarks by John W. Gardner Made to the National Association of Schools of Public Affairs and Administration Conference, Seattle, Washington, October 23, 1987." In *Public Enterprise: A Newsletter of the National Association of Schools of Public Affairs and Administration* (December).

Gawthrop, Louis C. 1984. *Public Sector Management, Systems and Ethics*. Bloomington: Indiana University Press.

Goodnow, F. J. 1900. *Politics and Administration: A Study in Government*. New York: Russell and Russell. Reissued in 1967.

Goodsell, Charles T. 1988. *The Social Meaning of Civic Space*. Lawrence: University Press of Kansas.

———. 1990. "Public Administration and the Public Interest." In *Refounding Public Administration*, ed. Gary L. Wamsley et al., pp. 96–113. Beverly Hills: Sage.

Graves, W. Brooke. 1964. *American Intergovernmental Relations: Their Origins, Historical Development, and Current Status*. New York: Charles Scribner's Sons.

Greenstein, Fred I. 1988. "Nine Presidents in Search of the Modern Presidency." In *Leadership in the Modern Presidency*, ed. Greenstein, pp. 296–352. Cambridge, Mass.: Harvard University Press.

Grossman, Michael Baruch, and Martha Joynt Kumar. 1981. *Portraying the President: The White House and the Media*. Baltimore: Johns Hopkins University Press.

Gulick, Luther, and Lyndall Urwick, eds. 1937. *Papers on the Science of Administration*. New York: Institute of Public Administration.

Haas, Peter J., and Deil S. Wright. 1989. "Public Policymaking and Administrative Turnover in State Government: The Role of the Governor." *Policy Studies Journal* 17 (Summer): 788–803.

———. Forthcoming. "Administrative Turnover in State Government: A Research Note." *Administration and Society*.

Haber, Samuel. 1964. *Efficiency and Uplift: Scientific Management in the Progressive Era, 1890–1920.* Chicago: University of Chicago Press.

Haga, William J. 1974. "Perils of Professionalism." *Management Quarterly* (September): 3–10.

Halberstam, David. 1972. *The Best and the Brightest.* New York: Random House.

Hamilton, Chris, and Donald Wells. 1990. *Federalism, Power and Political Economy: A New Theory of Federalism and Its Impact on American Life.* Englewood Cliffs, N.J.: Prentice-Hall.

Hanus, Jerome J., ed. 1981. *The Nationalization of the States.* Lexington, Mass.: D. C. Heath.

Hargrove, Edwin C., and Michael Nelson. 1984. *Presidents, Politics, and Policy.* New York: Knopf.

Hart, John. 1987. *The Presidential Branch.* Elmsford, N.Y.: Pergamon Press.

Hart, Lois Borland. 1980. *Moving Up: Women and Leadership.* New York: AMACOM.

Hastedt, Glen P. 1985. "The United States Response to Direct Foreign Investments, 1973–1974." *Southeastern Political Review* 13: 39–64.

Hebert, F. Ted, Jeffrey L. Brudney, and Deil S. Wright. 1983. "Gubernatorial Influence and the State Bureaucracy." *American Politics Quarterly* 11 (Fall): 243–64.

Heclo, Hugh. 1984. "Executive Budget Making." In *Federal Budget Policy in the 1980s*, ed. Gregory B. Mills and John Palmer, pp. 261–90. Washington, D.C.: Urban Institute Press.

Henig, Jeffrey. 1985. *Public Policy and Federalism: Issues in State and Local Politics.* New York: St. Martin's Press.

Hero, Rodney E. 1986. "The Urban Service Delivery Literature: Some Questions and Considerations." *Polity* 18 (Summer): 659–77.

Herzik, Eric B., and Mary L. Dodson. 1982. "The President and Public Expectations: A Research Note." *Presidential Studies Quarterly* 12 (Spring): 168–73.

Hess, Stephen. 1988. *Organizing the Presidency.* Rev. ed. Washington, D.C.: Brookings Institution.

Hinckley, Barbara. 1985. *Problems of the Presidency: A Text with Readings.* Glenview, Ill.: Scott, Foresman.

House, Robert J. 1977. "A 1976 Theory of Charismatic Leadership." In *Leadership: The Cutting Edge*, ed. James G. Hunt and Lars L. Larson, pp. 189–207. Carbondale: Southern Illinois University Press.

Housewright, Edward. 1988. "Council Criticizes Fee Hike at Pools." *Dallas Morning News* (September 9): 26A.

Hummel, Ralph R. 1987. *The Bureaucratic Experience.* 3d ed. New York: St. Martin's Press.

Jones, Charles O., ed. 1988. *The Reagan Legacy: Promise and Performance.* Chatham, N.J.: Chatham House.

Jones, Charles O., and Robert D. Thomas, eds. 1976. *Public Policy Making in the Federal System.* Bevery Hills: Sage.

Kallenbach, Joseph E. 1966. *The American Chief Executive: The Presidency and the Governorship.* New York: Harper & Row.

Kaufman, Herbert. 1960. *The Forest Ranger*. Baltimore: Johns Hopkins University Press.

Kearney, Richard C., and Chandan Sinha. 1988. "Professionalism and Bureaucratic Responsiveness: Conflict or Compatibility?" *Public Administration Review* 48 (May–June): 571–79.

Kearns, Doris. 1972. *Lyndon Johnson and the American Dream*. New York: Harper & Row.

Keegan, John. 1987. *The Mask of Command*. Harrisonburg, Va.: R. R. Donnelley & Sons.

Kerbel, Matthew R. 1986. "Against the Odds: Media Access in the Administration of President Ford." *Presidential Studies Quarterly* 16 (Winter): 76–91.

Kernell, Samuel. 1986. *Going Public: New Strategies of Presidential Leadership*. Washington, D.C.: CQ Press.

Kernell, Samuel, and Samuel Popkin. 1986. *Chief of Staff*. Berkeley and Los Angeles: University of California Press.

King, Anthony, ed. 1978. *The New American Political System*. Washington, D.C.: American Enterprise Institute.

———. 1983. *State Government Influence in U.S. International Economic Policy*. Lexington, Mass.: Lexington Books.

Kline, John M. 1984. "The International Economic Interests of the States." *Publius* 14 (Fall): 81–94.

———. 1983. *State Government Influence in U.S. International Economic Policy*. Lexington, Mass.: Lexington Books.

Knott, James H., and Gerald J. Miller. 1987. *Reforming Bureaucracy: The Politics of Institutional Choice*. Englewood Cliffs, N.J.: Prentice-Hall.

Kotlikoff, Laurence J. 1987. "Budget Deficits, Stripped of Delusions." *Wall Street Journal* (November 4): 6.

Laski, Harold J. 1949. *The American Democracy: A Commentary and an Interpretation*. London: Allen & Unwin.

Leakachman, Robert. 1982. *Greed Is Not Enough: Reaganomics*. New York: Pantheon Books.

Leys, Wayne A. R. 1952. *Ethics for Policy Decisions*. New York: Prentice-Hall.

Light, Paul. 1982. *The President's Agenda*. Baltimore: Johns Hopkins University Press.

———. 1984. *Vice-Presidential Power*. Baltimore: Johns Hopkins University Press.

Lippmann, Walter. 1955. *Essays in the Public Philosophy*. Boston: Little, Brown.

Lipset, Seymour Martin, and William Schneider. 1983. *The Confidence Gap in the Public Mind: Business, Labor, and Government in the Public Mind*. New York: Free Press.

Lipson, Leslie. 1939. *The American Governor: From Figurehead to Leader*. Chicago: University of Chicago Press.

Lowi, Theodore J. 1969. *The End of Liberalism*. New York: Norton.

McCloskey, Robert G., ed. 1962. *Essays in Constitutional Law*. New York: Knopf.

McCubbins, Mathew D., and Thomas Schwartz. 1984. "Congressional Oversight Overlooked: Police Patrols versus Fire Alarms." *American Journal of Political Science* 38 (February): 165–77.

McMurty, Virginia. 1986. "OMB's Role in the Federal Budget Process." In *Office of Management and Budget: Evolving Roles and Future Issues*, prepared by the Congressional Research Service, Library of Congress, pp. 1–72. Washington, D.C.: U.S. Government Printing Office.

Mann, Thomas, and Norman Ornstein. 1981. *The New Congress*. Washington, D.C.: American Enterprise Institute.

Manning, Bayless. 1977. "The Congress, the Executive and Intermestic Affairs." *Foreign Affairs* 55 (January): 306–24.

Margolis, Stewart. 1988. Letter to the Editor, *Los Angeles Times* (August 8): II-4.

Martin, Roscoe C. 1965. *The Cities and the Federal System*. New York: Atherton Press.

Maslow, Abraham H. 1970. *Motivation and Personality*. New York: Harper & Row.

Mathews, David. 1984. "The Public in Theory and Practice." *Public Administration Review* 44 (March): 122–23.

Meier, Kenneth J. 1980. "Executive Reorganization of Government: Impact on Employment and Expenditures." *American Journal of Political Science* 24 (August): 396–412.

Melanson, Richard A., and David Mayers, eds. 1987. *Reevaluating Eisenhower: American Foreign Policy in the 1950's*. Urbana: University of Illinois Press.

Miller, Cheryl M. 1987. "The Politics of Legislative Curtailment of Administrative Rulemaking: Obstacles to Police-Patrol Oversight." *Policy Studies Review* 6 (May): 631–44.

Millerson, Geoffrey. 1964. *The Qualifying Associations*. London: Routledge & Kegan Paul.

Mitchell, Terrence R., and William G. Scott. 1987. "Leadership Failure, the Distrusting Public, and Prospects of the Administrative State." *Public Administration Review* 47 (November–December): 445–52.

Moe, Terry M. 1985. "The Politicized Presidency." In *The New Direction in American Politics*, ed. John E. Chubb and Paul E. Peterson, pp. 235–72. Washington, D.C.: Brookings Institution.

Mooney, James D. 1937. "The Principles of Organization." In *Papers on the Science of Administration*, ed. Luther Gulick and Lyndall Urwick, pp. 91–98. New York: Institute of Public Administration.

Mosher, Frederick C. 1968. *Democracy and the Public Service*. New York: Oxford University Press.

Murchland, Bernard. 1983. "Thinking about the Public." *Kettering Review* (Winter): 11–17.

Nathan, Richard. 1983. *The Administrative Presidency*. New York: Wiley.

National Governors Association. 1978. *Governing the American States: A Handbook for Governors*. Washington, D.C.: National Governors Association, Center for Policy Research.

Newell, Charldean, and David N. Ammons. 1987. "Role Emphases of City Managers and Other Municipal Executives." *Public Administration Review* 47 (May–June): 246–53.

Newland, Chester A. 1984. "Executive Office Policy Apparatus: Enforcing the Reagan Agenda." In *The Reagan Presidency and the Governing of America*, ed. Lester M.

Salamon and Michael Lund, pp. 135–68. Washington, D.C.: Urban Institute Press.

Ornstein, Norman J. 1983. "The Open Congress Meets the President." In *Both Ends of the Avenue*, ed. Anthony King, pp. 185–211. Washington, D.C.: American Enterprise Institute.

Ornstein, Norman J., Andrew Kohut, and Larry McCarthy. 1988. *The People, the Press, and Politics*. Reading, Mass.: Addison-Wesley.

Ostrom, Vincent. 1976. "The Contemporary Debate over Centralization and Decentralization." *Publius* 6 (Fall): 21–32.

Palmer, John L., and Isabel V. Sawhill. 1985. *The Reagan Record*. Washington, D.C.: Urban Institute Press.

Palmer, Parker J. 1981. *The Company of Strangers: Christians and the Renewal of America's Public Life*. New York: Crossroads.

———. 1984. "The Nature and Nurture of Public Life." *Kettering Review* (Fall): 46–55.

Perrow, Charles. 1977. "Three Types of Effectiveness Studies." In *New Perspectives on Organizational Effectiveness*, ed. Paul S. Goodman and Johannes Pennings, pp. 96–105. San Francisco: Jossey-Bass.

Peterson, Paul E. 1985. "The New Politics of Deficits." In *The New Direction in American Politics*, ed. John E. Chubb and Paul E. Peterson, pp. 365–97. Washington, D.C.: Brookings Institution.

Pfiffner, James F. 1988. *The Strategic Presidency*. Chicago: Dorsey Press.

———. 1990. "Establishing the Bush Presidency." *Public Administration Review* 50 (January–February): 64–73.

Polsby, Nelson W., and Aaron Wildavsky. 1984. *Presidential Elections: Strategies of American Politics*. 6th ed. New York: Charles Scribner's Sons.

Posner, Alan R. 1984. *State Government Export Promotion: An Exporter's Guide*. Westport, Conn.: Quorum Books.

Price, Don K. 1965. *The Scientific Estate*. Cambridge, Mass.: Harvard University Press.

Rainey, Hal G., and Robert W. Rackoff. 1982. "Professionals in Public Organizations: Organizational Environments and Incentives." *American Review of Public Administration* 16 (Winter): 319–35.

Ransone, Coleman B., Jr. 1956. *The Office of the Governor in the United States*. Tuscaloosa: University of Alabama Press.

———. 1982. *The American Governorship*. Westport, Conn.: Greenwood Press.

Reagan, Ronald. 1982. "Text of President's Message to the Nation." *New York Times* (January 27): A16.

Reedy, George E. 1982. *Lyndon B. Johnson: A Memoir*. New York: Andrews and McMeel.

Reich, Robert B. 1985. "Public Administration and Public Deliberation: An Interpretive Essay." *Yale Law Journal* 94 (June): 1617–41.

Reichard, Gary W. 1975. *The Reaffirmation of Republicanism*. Knoxville: University of Tennessee Press.

Richardson, Elmo. 1979. *The Presidency of Dwight D. Eisenhower*. Lawrence: Regents Press of Kansas.

Ridley, Clarence E., and O. F. Nolting. 1934. *The City Manager Profession.* Chicago: University of Chicago Press.

Rockman, Bert A. 1984. *The Leadership Question: The Presidency and the American System.* New York: Praeger.

Rose, Richard. 1988. *The Postmodern President: The White House Meets the World.* Chatham, N.J.: Chatham House.

Rosenberg, Morton. 1986. "Regulatory Management at OMB." In *Office of Management and Budget: Evolving Roles and Future Issues,* prepared by Congressional Research Service, Library of Congress, pp. 185–234. Washington, D.C.: U.S. Government Printing Office.

Rosenbloom, David H. 1987. "Public Administration and the Judiciary: The 'New Partnership.'" *Public Administration Review* 48 (January–February): 75–83.

———. 1988. "The Public Employment Relationship and the Supreme Court in the 1980s." *Review of Public Personnel Administration* 48 (Spring): 49–65.

Rubin, Richard. 1981. *Press, Party, and Presidency.* New York: Norton.

Sabato, Larry. 1983. *Goodbye to Good-Time Charlie: The American Governorship Transformed.* 2d ed. Lexington, Mass.: D. C. Heath.

Safire, William. 1982. "The New New Federalism Is Bolder." *Birmingham Post-Herald* (January 29): A5.

Sanford, Terry. 1967. *Storm over the States.* New York: McGraw-Hill.

Schaar, John H. 1969. "Legitimacy in the Modern State." In *Power and Community: Dissenting Essays in Political Science,* ed. Philip Green and Sanford Levinson, pp. 278–317. New York: Random House.

Schein, Edgar H. 1985. *Organizational Culture and Leadership.* San Francisco: Jossey-Bass.

Schick, Alan. 1984. "The Budget as an Instrument of Presidential Policy." In *The Reagan Presidency and the Governing of America,* ed. Lester M. Salamon and Michael Lund, pp. 91–125. Washington, D.C.: Urban Institute Press.

Schlesinger, Joseph A. 1965. "The Politics of the Executive." In *Politics in the American States: A Comparative Analysis,* ed. Herbert Jacob and Kenneth N. Vines, pp. 207–37. Boston: Little, Brown.

Schmandt, Jurgen, and Hilliard Roderick. 1985. *Acid Rain and Friendly Neighbors: The Policy Dispute between Canada and the United States.* Durham, N.C.: Duke University Press.

Schon, Donald. 1971. *Beyond the Stable State.* New York: Norton.

Schubert, Glendon A. 1960. *The Public Interest.* Glencoe, Ill.: Free Press.

Sennett, Richard. 1977. *The Fall of Public Man.* New York: Knopf.

Sergiovani, Thomas J. 1979. "Is Leadership the Next Great Training Robbery?" *Educational Leadership* 30 (March): 388–94.

Shannon, John. 1988. "The Faces of Fiscal Federalism." *Intergovernmental Perspective* 14 (Winter): 15–17.

Sharp, Elaine B. 1986. *Citizen Demand-Making in the Urban Context.* Tuscaloosa: University of Alabama Press.

Sigelman, Lee, and Roland Smith. 1981. "Personal, Office, and State Characteristics as Predictors of Gubernatorial Performance." *Journal of Politics* 43 (May): 169–80.

Smith, Hedrick. 1982. "The President as Coalition Builder: Reagan's First Year." In *Rethinking the Presidency*, ed. Thomas E. Cronin, pp. 271–86. Boston: Little, Brown.

———. 1988. "Considerations on the Power System." *Presidential Studies Quarterly* 18 (Summer): 493–99.

Smoller, Fred. 1986. "The Six O'Clock Presidency: Patterns of Network News Coverage of the President." *Presidential Studies Quarterly* 16 (Winter): 31–49.

Sprengel, Donald P. 1972. "Governors' Staffs—Background and Recruitment Patterns." In *The American Governor in Behavioral Perspective*, ed. Thad L. Beyle and J. Oliver Williams, pp. 106–18. New York: Harper & Row.

Starr, Chauncey. 1969. "Social Benefit versus Technological Risk." *Science* 165: 1231–380.

Stone, Harold A., Don K. Price, and Kathryn H. Stone. 1940. *City Manager Government in the United States: A Review after Twenty-five Years*. Chicago: Public Administration Service.

Strong, Robert A. 1986. "Recapturing Leadership: The Carter Administration and the Crisis of Confidence." *Presidential Studies Quarterly* 16 (Fall): 636–50.

Sullivan, William M. 1982. *Reconstructing Public Philosophy*. Berkeley and Los Angeles: University of California Press.

Sundquist, James L. 1969. *Making Federalism Work*. Washington, D.C.: Brookings Institution.

"Text of President's Message to the Nation." 1982. *New York Times* (January 27): A16.

Thomas, John C. 1986. *Between Citizen and City*. Lawrence: University Press of Kansas.

Tipton, Howard D. 1989. "Response to 'The Nature of City Managers' Work.'" In *Ideal and Practice in Council [sic] Manager Government*, ed. H. George Frederickson, pp. 177–78. Washington, D.C.: International City Management Association.

U.S. Advisory Commission on Intergovernmental Relations. 1985. *The Question of State Government Capability*. Washington, D.C.: The Commission.

———. 1988. "A View from the Commission." *Intergovernmental Perspective* 14 (Summer): 2.

U.S. Bureau of the Census. 1990. *Public Employment in 1989*. Washington, D.C.: U.S. Bureau of the Census.

U.S. Congress. House. Committee on Energy and Commerce. 1981. *Presidential Control of Agency Rulemaking*. 97th Cong., 1st sess. Committee Print.

———. Committee on Rules. 1984. *Legislative Veto after Chadha*. Hearings before the Committee on Rules, 98th Cong., 2d Sess.

U.S. v. Cruikshank. 1876. 92 U.S. 542.

Upson, Lent D. 1915. "Comment on the Dayton Charter." In *City Manager Plan of Government*, ed. E. C. Mabie (1918), pp. 59–65. New York: Wilson Company. Reprinted from *National Municipal Review* 4 (April): 266–72.

Urwick, Lyndall. 1937. "Organization as a Technical Problem." In *Papers on the Science of Administration*, ed. Luther Gulick and Lyndall Urwick, pp. 49–88. New York: Institute of Public Administration.

Waldo, Dwight. 1948. *The Administrative State*. New York: Ronald Press.

Wamsley, Gary L., et al. 1990. *Refounding Public Administration*. Beverly Hills: Sage.

Washington Post. 1988. August 17: A1c.

Weinberg, Louise. 1977. "The New Judicial Federalism." *Stanford Law Review* 29 (July): 1191–94.

Weinberg, Martha Wagner. 1977. *Managing the State.* Cambridge, Mass.: MIT Press.

Weissert, Carol S. 1980. "ACIR and the Intergovernmental System: A 20-Year Review." *Intergovernmental Perspective* 6 (Winter): 14–23.

Wells, Donald T. 1987. "The Nationalization of the States: Partial Preemption and Hazardous Waste Policy." *Social Sciences Perspectives Journal* 2: 136–50.

West, William, and Joseph Cooper. 1985. "The Rise of Administrative Clearance." In *The Presidency and Public Policy Making,* ed. George C. Edwards III, Steven Shull, and Norman Thomas, pp. 192–214. Pittsburgh: University of Pittsburgh Press.

Whicker, Marcia Lynn, and Raymond A. Moore. 1988. *When Presidents Are Great.* Englewood Cliffs, N.J.: Prentice-Hall.

White, Leonard D. 1926. *Introduction to the Study of Public Administration.* New York: Macmillan.

———. 1927. *The City Manager.* Chicago: University of Chicago Press.

———. 1953. *The States and the Nation.* Baton Rouge: Louisiana State University Press.

White, Orion. 1981. "The Citizen of the 1980's." In *The Public Encounter,* ed. Charles T. Goodsell, pp. 206–19. Bloomington: Indiana University Press.

Will, George F. 1983. *Statecraft as Soulcraft: What Government Does.* New York: Simon and Schuster.

Willner, Ann R. 1984. *The Spellbinders: Charismatic Political Leadership—A Theory.* New Haven: Yale University Press.

Willoughby, William F. 1927. *Principles of Public Administration.* Washington, D.C.: Brookings Institution.

Wright, Deil S. N.d. *American State Administrators Project.* Chapel Hill, N.C.: Institute for Research in Social Science, University of North Carolina.

———. 1967. "Executive Leadership and State Administration." *Midwest Journal of Political Science* 11 (February): 1–20.

———. 1978. *Understanding Intergovernmental Relations.* 1st ed. North Scituate, Mass.: Duxbury Press.

———. 1982. *Understanding Intergovernmental Relations.* 2d ed. Monterey: Brooks/Cole.

———. 1988. *Understanding Intergovernmental Relations.* 3d ed. Pacific Grove, Calif.: Brooks/Cole.

———. 1990. "Information and Introductory Materials on the American State Administrators Project." Department of Political Science, University of North Carolina.

Wrightson, Margaret. 1986. "Interlocal Cooperation and Urban Problems: Lessons from the New Federalism." *Urban Affairs Quarterly* 22 (December): 261–75.

Wyner, Alan J. 1972. "Staffing the Governor's Office." In *The American Governor in Behavioral Perspective,* ed. Thad L. Beyle and J. Oliver Williams, pp. 118–25. New York: Harper & Row.

Younger v. Harris. 1971. 401 U.S. 37.

Zaleznik, Abraham. 1977. "Managers and Leaders: Are They Different?" *Harvard Business Review* (May–June): 67–78.

CONTRIBUTORS

TODD W. ARESON occupies a position on the faculty of the School of Public and Environmental Affairs at Indiana University–South Bend. Besides prior academic experience, he has also worked with organizations of local officials, including the National League of Cities and the International City Management Association. Recently he was coeditor, with Marcia Whicker, of *Public Sector Management.*

RYAN J. BARILLEAUX, currently an associate professor of political science at Miami University (Ohio), was formerly an aide to Senator J. Bennett Johnston. His articles dealing with the presidency and American politics have appeared in a variety of scholarly journals. He is also coauthor of *The President as World Leader.*

ROBERT B. DENHARDT is professor of public administration in the School of Public Affairs at the University of Central Florida. He is a recent past president of the American Society for Public Administration, was the founder of ASPA's National Campaign for Public Service, and has to his credit more than fifty scholarly publications, most recently the book *Public Administration: An Action Orientation.*

H. GEORGE FREDERICKSON is the Stene Distinguished Professor of Public Administration at the University of Kansas. He formerly served as president of Eastern Washington University. The author of numerous scholarly publications, he has been recognized by his peers with the presidency of the American Society for Public Administration and, most recently, the distinguished research award of ASPA and the National Association of Schools of Public Affairs and Administration. Currently, he serves as editor of the *Journal of Public Administration Research and Theory.*

CHARLES T. GOODSELL is professor and director of the Center for Public Administration and Policy, Virginia Polytechnic Institute and State University. He has written numerous publications, including *The Social Meaning of Civic Space* and *The Case for Bureaucracy*. He has also held teaching positions at Texas, Southern Illinois, Puerto Rico, and Carleton.

CHERYL M. MILLER is associated with the policy sciences graduate program at the University of Maryland, Baltimore County, and is a member of the faculty of the university's political science department. She has published prominently in the areas of administrative rule making and the policy influence of state legislative black caucuses.

JOHN NALBANDIAN developed his interest in professional leadership in local governing during the five years he served as chair of the Department of Public Administration at the University of Kansas, where he continues as a faculty member. He is coauthor of *Public Personnel Management* and has a manuscript in preparation on better city management.

KEVIN PRELGOVISK is an administrative analyst with the Long Beach, California, city government. Before he received his M.P.A., he spent several years in East Africa with the U.S. Peace Corps and Lutheran World Relief.

WILLIAM H. STEWART is a professor of political science at the University of Alabama. He is also director of the doctoral program in public administration offered by the University at Maxwell Air Force Base. He has numerous research interests, ranging from federalism on a world scale to Alabama state and local politics, the subject of his most recent coauthored book.

DONALD T. WELLS heads the Department of Political Science at West Georgia College in which he also holds the rank of professor. His primary areas of research have been the American federal system and public policy, particularly environmental policy. Most recently he coauthored *Federalism, Power, and Political Economy*. For a dozen years he was editor of the *Southeastern Political Review*.

MARCIA LYNN WHICKER is on the faculty of the Department of Public Administration at Virginia Commonwealth University. She has also been a member of the faculties of Temple, Wayne State, and South Carolina. She has numerous publications to her credit in leading scholarly journals. Most recently, she has done extensive lecturing and writing on presidential leadership.

DEIL S. WRIGHT is Alumni Distinguished Professor of Political Science at the University of North Carolina, Chapel Hill. He is the author of more than sixty articles that have appeared in leading journals in his fields of research. His book *Understanding Intergovernmental Relations* is now in its third edition.

INDEX

Abney, Glenn, 102, 104
Adams, Sherman, 75
Administration: defined, 20; clearance, 50, 52, 62; rule making, 50; accountability, 140–41
Agnew, Spiro, 79
Amateurism, 16
American Governorship, The (Ransone), 2
Ammons, David N., 138
Anderson, Martin, 59
Areson, Todd W., 5, 64–80, 155, 158, 159–60
Arms Control and Disarmament Act, 48

Balanced Budget Act, 49
Barber, Bernard, 11
Barber, James D., 78
Barilleaux, Ryan J., 4, 45–63, 154–55, 157
Bellah, Robert N., 26–27
Bennis, Warren, 35, 39, 43
Beyle, Thad L., 103
Block grants, 84
Brennan, William, 54
Brown v. *Board of Education*, 75
Bryce, James, 119, 136
Budget, 60–62

Burger, Warren, 83
Burns, James MacGregor, 35, 36, 37, 43–44
Bush, George, 46–47, 50, 51, 55, 56, 60–61, 64, 65, 67, 68–69, 70, 71, 72

Carlucci, Frank, 17
Carter, Jimmy, 46, 49, 51, 53, 54, 55, 61, 65, 68, 69, 70, 71, 74, 79–80
Case Act, 47, 48
Chief of staff, 57
Childs, Richard S., 142, 143, 144
City managers, 6, 137–51; evolution of role, 137–39; policy orientation, 138ff; qualifications, 138–39; foundations, 139–43; depoliticization of, 142–43; vulnerability, 143–44. *See also* Council-manager plan
Cleveland, Harlan, 39, 43, 44
Cognitive resource theory, 34
Company of strangers, 29–30, 31
Congressional Budget and Impoundment Act, 47, 49
Cooke, Alistair, 70
Cooperative federalism, 5, 82, 85–87, 88, 89, 90, 91
Council-manager plan, 6; weaknesses, 143–44; legitimacy, 144–46. *See also* City managers

Daley, Richard, 18
Darman, Richard, 49
Denhardt, Robert B., 4, 33–44, 153–60
Dever, John, 138
Dewey, John, 23
Dewey, Thomas E., 77
Downs, Anthony, 95
Downs, Thomas, 147
Dual federalism, 5, 82–85, 86, 87
Dukakis, Michael, 65

Efficiency, 141–42
Eisenhower, Dwight D., 53, 68, 74,
  75–76, 77
Elazar, Daniel J., 125
Ethics, 16–17
Executive Office of the President, 4,
  51–53, 57, 63

Federalism: and administrative discre-
  tion, 81–94; relevance to executive
  leadership, 82; models, 5, 155
Fiedler, Fred E., 34
Fireside Chats, 74, 79
Fiscal federalism, 132
Fischhoff, Baruch, 159
Ford, Gerald, 46, 55, 70, 79
Forrestal, James, 2
Frederickson, H. George, 4, 20–32, 154,
  156–57, 158, 159

Gardner, John, 33
Gawthrop, Louis, 27–28
General secretariat, 51, 57, 58
Gleason, Michael, 149–50
Goldwater, Barry, 49
Goldwater v. Carter, 49
Goodnow, Frank J., 143
Goodsell, Charles T., 3–4, 7–19, 30,
  153, 156, 160
Governor: roles, 2, 102; relation to leg-
  islature, 5; areas of leadership, 5; and
  state administration, 95–118; growth
  in power, 101; staff, 102–3; formal
  powers, 103–5; institutionalization,

105; oversight of administration,
  108–17; comparative influence,
  109–15; formative period, 119–20;
  and public policy, 119–36; modernization, 120; classification, 128; as
  policy leader, 132–36; as partisan,
  134–35; "new breed," 135–36
Gulick, Luther, 142

Haber, Samuel, 141, 143
Haga, William J., 11
Hazardous waste policy, 122
Honeymoon period, 64, 65
Hoover, Herbert, 65, 78
Hoover, J. Edgar, 16

Imperial Presidency, 46
INS v. Chadha, 48–49
Iran-Contra affair, 14, 58
Iranian hostage crisis, 79

Jackson, Andrew, 124
Johnson, Lyndon B., 46, 53, 64, 71, 76,
  88, 89

Kaufman, Herbert, 92
Kearney, Richard C., 12
Kennedy, John F., 46, 53, 64, 67, 68, 70,
  71, 73, 74
"KISS" theory, 66
Kline, John M., 129
Kotlikoff, Laurence, 127

Laski, Harold, 120
Lauth, Thomas P., 102, 104
Leadership: studies of, 34–35; defined,
  34; traits, 35; types, 35; and power,
  36–37; as an aspect of social development, 36–37; as a process, 37;
  harmful, 38; and the developmental
  process, 40–43; education for, 40–43;
  transformational, 72
Legislative veto, 48–49
Light, Paul, 60
Lippmann, Walter, 23

Lipset, Seymour, 33
Lipson, Leslie, 101–2, 119, 120
Lowi, Theodore J., 123
Low Level Nuclear Waste Act, 122

MacArthur, Douglas, 16
Madison, James, 119
Managerialism, 16
Manahan, Jack, 148
Margolis, Stewart, 148
Marshall, George C., 15
Marshall Plan, 76
Martin, Roscoe, 89
Maslow, Abraham, 68
Mathews, David, 21, 22, 25
Meese, Edwin, 85
Miller, Cheryl M., 5, 95–118, 154,
    155–56, 158
Millerson, Geoffrey, 11
Mitchell, Terrence R., 33
Mondale, Walter, 55
Mosher, Frederick, 8
Muchmore, Lynn R., 103, 104
Murchland, Bernard, 28

Nalbandian, John, 6, 137–51, 157, 158,
    159
Nanus, Bert, 35
Nathan, Richard, 59
National Commitments Resolution, 47
National federalism, 5, 82, 87–90
National Security Council, 52–53
Neustadt, Richard, 74
Newell, Charldean, 137–38
New federalism, 5, 82, 90–93, 132
New judicial federalism, 83
Nixon, Richard M., 5, 17, 46, 51, 52,
    53, 58, 59, 69, 71, 77–78, 79, 82, 83,
    90–92, 93

Office of Governor in the South, The
    (Ransone), 2
Office of Governor in the United
    States, The (Ransone), 2

Office of Management and Budget, 49,
    50, 52; Legislative Reference Divi-
    sion, 52
Operational federalism, 81
Ornstein, Norman, 54
Ostrom, Vincent, 90

Palmer, Parker, 21, 24, 29, 31
Parallel unilateral policy declarations
    (PUPD), 48, 62
Partial preemption, 122
Perrow, Charles, 121
Persian Gulf War, 48
Pfiffner, James, 56
Policy making: vicarious, 53–54, 60;
    context of, 119–36
Political professionalism, 3–4, 6, 7–19;
    categories, 9; traits, 12–18
Politics-administration dichotomy, 9,
    12, 139–40
Positivism, 22–23, 25
Postimperial presidency, 46
Postmodern presidency, 4, 45–63, 155;
    features, 47–56
Power, 36–37
Pragmatism, 28
Prelgovisk, Kevin, 4, 33–44, 154, 157,
    158, 159
Prerogative power: revival, 47–50, 63;
    in foreign policy, 47–49; in budget-
    ing, 49; administrative clearance, 50
President: legislative leadership, 54–55;
    political strategy, 56–63; advice to,
    56–63; persuasiveness, 64–80; mes-
    sages, 65–69; as messenger, 69–72;
    model, 72–73; examples, 73–80
Price, Don K., 12
Private management, 38
Process politics, 135, 136
Profession: traditional ideas, 8–10; de-
    fined, 11–12; in local government,
    137–51. See also Political profession-
    alism
Progressive movement, 102
Project grants, 92

Public: defined, 20–32; contrasting perspectives, 23–25
Public administration: defined, 20–21, 25 passim; responsibilities and role, 25–29
Public choice theory, 26
Public interest, 25, 27; and efficiency, 141–42
Public leadership, 4, 33–44
Public policy: and intergenerational concern, 126–28; international scope, 128–29, 134; and intergovernmental relations, 130–32, 135. *See also* Policy making
Public politics, 50–51, 63

Quayle, Dan, 55, 65

Rackoff, Robert W., 11, 17
Ragsdale, Diane, 149
Rainey, Hal G., 11, 17
Ransone, Coleman B., Jr., 1–3, 5, 6, 7, 10, 18, 19, 81, 96, 97, 102, 103, 115, 121, 153, 156, 160
Reagan, Ronald, 5, 17, 46, 47–48, 49, 50, 51, 53, 55, 58, 59, 60–61, 62, 64–67, 68, 69, 70, 71, 72, 73, 74–75, 82, 84, 85, 90, 91, 92, 93
Regulatory federalism, 89, 124
Rehnquist, William, 53
Reich, Robert, 17–18
Resource Conservation and Recovery Act, 123, 130–31
Revenue sharing, 83–84, 90
Rockefeller, Nelson, 18, 55
Roosevelt, Franklin D., 45, 51, 65, 70, 71, 73–74, 75, 79, 83, 89
Ruckelshaus, William, 17
Rule of defensibility, 58

Sabato, Larry, 104, 105, 133
Safire, William, 90–91
Schaar, John, 146
Schlesinger, Joseph A., 104
Schneider, William, 33

Scott, William G., 33
Sennett, Richard, 23, 30–31
Shannon, John, 132
Sharp, Elaine, 145
Sherman, Roger, 134
Sinha, Chandan, 12
Sometime governments, 105
Souter, David, 54
Southern Regional Training Program in Public Administration (SRTP), 1, 2, 3, 4, 156
Sprengel, Donald P., 103
State administration: overview, 95–118; depth and diversity, 97–98; size, 97, 99; impact of federal aid, 98, 100–1; reform, 102
State legislatures: revitalization, 105; structure and procedures, 106–7; oversight of administration, 107, 108–17; comparative influence, 109–15
Stewart, William H., 5, 81–94, 153–60
Stockman, David, 49, 61
Sullivan, William, 24

Tipton, Howard, 138
Truman, Harry, 18, 71, 75, 76, 86

U.S. v. *Cruikshank*, 83
Urwick, Lyndall, 142
Utilitarian philosophy, 22–23, 24, 29, 31

Vice-President, 55–56, 57
Vietnam, 76

Wamsley, Gary, 18
War Powers Resolution, 47–48
Warren, Earl, 53, 75
Washington, George, 45
Watergate, 14, 17, 69, 78
Weinberg, Louise, 83
Wells, Donald T., 5, 119–35, 153–54, 157, 160
Whicker, Marcia Lynn, 5, 64–80, 155, 158, 159–60

White, Leonard, 140, 141, 143–44
White, Orion, 26
White House staff, 57
Will, George, 24–25
Wilson, Woodrow, 86
Wright, Deil S., 5, 87, 95–118, 138, 154, 155–56, 158

Wrightson, Margaret, 124–25
Wyner, Alan J., 103

Younger v. *Harris*, 83

Zaleznik, Abraham, 34